Also by Eric Blakebrough . . .

No Quick Fix
Called to be Giants
Permission to Be
Church for the City

CATCH THE WIND

A Journey in Faith

by

Eric Blakebrough

Hilton Mill Books

Published in 2012 by
Hilton Mill Books
Hilton Mill, Roch, Haverfordwest
Pembrokeshire, SA62 6AE

ISBN 978-0-9573134-0-8

Cover design: Myfanwy Franks

Printed in Wales by
Dinefwr Press Ltd., Rawlings Road, Llandybïe
Carmarthenshire, SA18 3YD

For Mary, my beloved wife

Preface

As we are approaching the 500th anniversary of the Reformation, can a former Baptist minister who has become a Roman Catholic, say anything to help Protestant and Catholics understand each other better? And, as an increasing number of people are alienated by church dogmas, does pastoral experience suggest some moulds need breaking, in order that the church may be of greater service to people today?

Hilton Mill   *Eric Blakebrough*
Roch   June 2012
Pembrokeshire

Contents

1.

Beginnings

There are three Blakebroughs in the Baptist Union Directory: Eric, ordained 1955; Adele, ordained 1984; Martin, ordained 1987. I doubt if it is a record for a daughter and a son to follow their father into the ministry, but it is unusual. Our eldest son, Justin after graduating and qualifying as a teacher, served with the Baptist Missionary Society in Zaire for 3 years. Our family has been nourished by the fellowship of Baptist churches and inspired by the Free Church tradition. Why then, after more than fifty years as an ordained Baptist Minister, have I become a Roman Catholic?

I spent most of my childhood separated from my parents and away from home. This had made me independent, self reliant and suspicious of authority. My parents, grandparents, uncles and aunts were all independent traders, self-employed, neither upper nor lower class; just the kind of people who are naturally nonconformist and, if they are religious, typically members of Free Churches. If they have a sense of Britishness, it is of the Protestant kind, inheritors of a version of history which repeatedly casts Catholics in the role of traitors. My family did not drink alcohol, did not gamble, and kept Sunday special. These simple virtues we did not associate with Catholics.

My relatives spoke with London accents, except my maternal grandmother who spoke with a soft voice and an attractive lilt. All my relatives loved me, but my grandmother also played with me. She made a tent in the garden. She cooked delicious cakes, puddings and tarts. A remarkable thing about my grandmother was that she danced in the garden. She used to tell me fairy stories, some were scary. But my beautiful grandmother died before she was old and before I was five. I cried for her for a long, long time.

My mother told me that my grandmother was Irish, born in Cork city. She had fled from Ireland when she was only 16 because of the grinding poverty. My auntie Rose, on my father's side, who was a Sunday School teacher at the Christian Brethren, explained to me that people in Ireland and other Catholic countries were poor because the priests told women that they must have as many babies as possible, even if they could not afford so many. Also, the priests took money from the poor to build elaborate churches, which is not what God wants. She told me that it can be shown in the Bible that the Pope is the Anti-Christ. She said that there are statues in Catholic churches which people bow down to, in direct contradiction to the Ten Commandments. No wonder my mother rejected Catholicism when she went with my father to the Christian Brethren when they were first married; although she had fond memories of her Convent school and of the nuns there, and she always gave up chocolates for Lent.

Let me describe the main features of my early life and of how I became an Evangelical Christian and a Baptist Minister.

I was evacuated from London at the age of eight, at the beginning of the last war. Prior to that, I had a happy childhood living with my parents in a new four bedroom house in Ilford, Essex. When they were first married, my parents attended the Christian Brethren, but by the time I left home they had lapsed. Their chief interest was their ideal home and garden. My father worked long hours as an electrician in order to realise their ambitions for themselves, for me and for my baby sister.

Evacuation for the duration of the war was an unhappy time for me. After the long train journey with other evacuee children, I arrived at dusk at a railway station in Suffolk and was taken to a village hall. Tired, dirty and hungry, 30 or so of us children were stood in front of an assembly of country folk to be selected for billeting. Before the selection process we were stripped nearly naked to be inspected for lice or other signs of disease. After this humiliation, host families chose who they wanted to stay with them. I was taller than the other children and thinner. Perhaps this was perceived as a possible symptom of T.B. which may explain why I was one of the last to be selected.

In bed in a strange house, I wet the bed. This was a valid reason for an evacuee being re-allocated to another family. After a series of unsuccessful placements I planned to run away and find my way home. I escaped back home to London on five separate occasions, and on each of these brief visits our house was bombed. The war was a traumatic experience for me.

I remember VE Day, Victory in Europe. By that time I had been evacuated to Northampton, and I remember everyone pouring on to the streets and into the Market Square. It was the first time I danced with a girl, or should I say jumped for joy like everyone else. The celebrations went on for several weeks.

With the ending of the war, most evacuees returned home to London, but during the last days of the war a V2 bomb had landed two or three houses away from our family home, causing serious damage. Builders were overstretched in the immediate post war period and it was about a year before I could return home.

My situation in Northampton was much better than before. The couple who took me into their home at the end of the war had always wanted a child of their own, and they were extremely kind. They had no notion of discipline and allowed me a great deal of personal freedom.

In my unrestricted leisure time I went to the cinema and one evening went to a performance of Gounod's Faust at the local theatre. From that first experience of Opera I became a devotee. On another evening, I met a man who took me to his house to show me his paintings and play the piano for me. The stranger who took me home was William Yeoman who, unbeknown to me at the time, was a Concert Hall pianist and a regular contributor to Radio programmes.

I had rarely been to school during my periods of evacuation, but the Northampton Education Authority caught up with me and allocated me a place at a London Grammar School which had been evacuated to the town. I was hopelessly behind in all academic subjects, but science lessons were taught at the North-ampton College of Technology where I found the laboratories exciting and enjoyed the practical lessons. In most classes at school I sat in misery, hoping the teacher would be compassionate enough not to notice me, but in the laboratories I was fully engaged. I hoped one day to be a scientist.

One Sunday afternoon as I walked down town, I noticed a poster outside the Northampton Central Hall announcing Gospel Services conducted by Rev. William Barker. Having nothing better to do, and curious to know why some people are religious, I noted the time and returned in the evening to attend the service. The Central Hall had originally been built for circus performances. It was in no sense a church building, and the audience of mainly elderly people looked somewhat out of place. They sang some hymns, heartily rather than tunefully, and there was a Bible reading and a prayer, but the clear purpose of the occasion was to hear the Reverend William Barker, who I assumed from the large poster outside was some kind of celebrity. I sat alone in the gallery, preferring not to be identified with the proceedings. I was just 16, in October 1945.

The Reverend Barker was a winsome man, in his early thirties. He wore a clerical collar, but having been a coal miner he had a down to earth manner of speaking. I cannot now recall any details of his message, but the theme is still clear in my memory. He gave examples of corruption in society and left us in no doubt about our part in that sin. Having convicted us all, he went on to glory in the infinite love and mercy of God. I do not remember in what way he expounded the place of the death of Christ in God's plan of salvation, but I do remember his assurance that we could all be forgiven and accepted by God. I tried to resist this gospel, but overwhelmingly I felt he preached the truth. I left the meeting without acknowledging anyone; I was in a state of acute anxiety not knowing what I was supposed to do.

During the next week, I found no relief from my anxiety. I tried to pray but felt no response. I resolved to go again the next Sunday, and I prayed that if God was really speaking to me he would make it clear what he wanted me to do.

On that next Sunday, William Barker spoke of the crucifixion of Christ being caused by man's sin. He spoke of Christ absorbing the sin of the world and of his death being a means of redemption. He used everyday language, but he seemed himself to enter into the passion of Christ as he made intercession to God to save all who called upon Jesus for salvation. I knew I had to make some response to God, but I needed someone to help me make that response. It was at this point that the preacher invited any to come forward who wanted to respond to God's love and mercy. I accepted the invitation, and from that moment until now I have never had any doubt about the validity of my encounter with God, that evening at the Central Hall in Northampton.

I knew from a conversation with my father that I had not been baptised as a baby, as my parents believed I should make my own decision on this matter when I was an adult. Now that I was an adult, especially since my religious experience at the Central Hall, I decided to be baptised. I spoke to the Rev. William Barker about my being baptised, and was astonished to learn that the Central Hall was not constituted as a church. It was an inter denominational mission, not attached to any particular denomination, and did not administer baptisms. He suggested I read various passages in the Bible and then we could decide how to proceed.

I read the account of the baptism of Jesus at the beginning of Mark's Gospel. Jesus was immersed in the river Jordan, and as he was coming up out of the water he saw the heavens open and the Spirit descending like a dove upon him. In Acts, chapter 2:37-41, I read that Peter preached to people, urging them to repent and be baptised. Then I came across a description of a baptism which seemed relevant to me. The Apostle Philip expounded the Christian Gospel to an Ethiopian court official, who responding, asked Philip to baptise him. The ceremony which is described took place at a roadside pool, large enough for the man to be immersed in the water (Acts 8:26-40). As I was about to return home to London, I postponed further consideration of the question of my baptism.

My home was in Ilford, and remembering a Sunday School I attended before the war, I went to the Claybury Park Baptist Church and spoke to the minister about my being baptised. Rev. Joseph Wilson explained that there was a baptistry under the floorboards, beneath the Communion Table, in the church. This was a rectangular tank large enough for a person to be immersed in water. This extraordinary structure corresponded to the pool the Ethiopian was baptised in, or the river Jesus was baptised in. Well, at least the mechanics for baptism were provided.

After a few weeks of instruction, and visitation by two Deacons to ascertain my faith, I was baptised at a Sunday service in the church. The minister in his sermon explained that baptism was a visible expression of spiritual regeneration (see John, chapter 3, and Romans, chapter 6). After prayer for the gift of the Holy Spirit, I was lead to the baptistry where the minister in a loud voice declared: "My brother, Eric, upon profession of your repentance towards God and faith in our Lord Jesus Christ, I baptise you in the name of the Father, and of the Son, and of the Holy Spirit. Amen." After being immersed, I came up out of the water as the congregation sang:

> O happy day, O happy day,
> when Jesus washed my sins away;
> he taught me how to watch and pray,
> and live rejoicing every day;
> O happy day, O happy day,
> when Jesus washed my sins away.

The New Testament describes three components in Christian initiation: repentance, belief and baptism. These are not intellectual concepts, they are workings of the Holy Spirit in a person's regeneration (see John, chapter 3). These belong together but in my case they were separated out somewhat. The work of repentance took place especially during that awful week after my first visit to the Central Hall and before my second visit. My acute anxiety then was a sense of estrangement from God and a conviction of guilt. The appeal to belief, came to me during the sermon on my second visit to the Central Hall. The preacher set before me the facts concerning the death of Jesus and the meaning of his sacrifice. In those moments of spiritual enlightenment I was 'there' before the cross where Jesus bore my sins in his body. When I was baptised, the Holy Spirit incorporated me into the death and resurrection of Christ, and this was manifested to me in the tears of joy I shed as I came up out of the water, while the congregation sang, O happy day!

Immediately after his baptism, Jesus was driven by the Holy Spirit into the wilderness where he underwent a period of testing prior to the beginning of his public ministry. I was not aware at the time of any parallel in my own life, but I now see a familiar pattern. As I began to think of my future, I felt that God was calling me to some kind of evangelical ministry, probably as a Baptist Minister, but I was not yet ready to make that commitment. I needed a period of testing, of toughening up! That is why I decided, in advance of conscription, to join the RAF at the age of 17 as a regular on a contract of eight years service, plus four years on reserve.

This was not an easy decision for me. Although I had spent most of the war separated from my parents, I was quite a solitary person from an aspiring middle class family with conventional values. I was not going into the RAF as an officer, but as an aircraftsman. I simply felt this was something I had to do before committing myself to any form of Christian ministry.

The first twelve weeks of basic training, known as square bashing, is at least as bad as purgatory, if not hell! After this, I was given eighteen months training as a Radar Fitter. At the end of this time, I was promoted to Corporal and posted to Technical Training Command as a Radar Instructor at the Advanced Ground Radar School at RAF Yatesbury. During my time in the RAF I tried to witness to my Christian faith in my personal life. I met other Evangelical Christians and we formed the RAF Gospel Team, preaching at weekends in the open air, in churches, or in other venues. The RAF was popular with the public in the immediate post war period, and our uniforms attracted large numbers of young females to our events!

These engagements confirmed that I had some gift for preaching and encouraged me to enquire about theological training. After a series of interviews by the Baptist Union Area Superintendent, representatives of the London Baptist Association and members of the Baptist Union Ministerial Committee, I was recommended for training at the Bristol Baptist College, but as yet I was only part way through my contract of service in the RAF. That is why I asked to see my Commanding Officer to request permission to buy myself out of the RAF in order to go into Holy Orders.

I stood to attention in front of the Officer's desk. The Commanding Officer was uncomfortable. He was considering my request for permission to buy myself out on the grounds of a Call to Holy Orders. The C.O. conferred with the Adjutant. He knew that in cases of venereal diseases men should be discharged. He knew that service women who became pregnant should be discharged. But he had never before been presented with a case of a Call to Holy Orders.

The Adjutant confirmed that Holy Orders could be grounds for permitting an airman to leave the Service. The C.O. hesitated for a moment or two, no doubt contemplating what would happen if half the men on the camp suddenly discovered they had a Call to Holy Orders.

"Corporal!"

"Sir!"

"Apropos your request to buy yourself out of the RAF to go into Holy Orders; it has not gone unnoticed that you are somewhat religious; I judge that this is a genuine case; permission granted upon the payment of eighty pounds."

"Thank you, Sir."

"And Corporal . . ."

"Sir?"

"I want you off this camp before 23.59 hours today! You are to pay eighty pounds to the Warrant Officer, hand in your uniform and kit, and check out at the Guard Room. You will be on indefinite leave until your discharge papers are sent to you. And Corporal . . ."

"Sir?"

"I don't want any more cases of Holy Orders, you understand?"

I saluted smartly, stamped my feet hard on the floor as I about turned and marched out of the office. Four hours later, having handed in my uniform, rifle and other kit, I stood outside the camp in my civilian clothes hitch hiking a lift on my way to the Bristol Baptist College to begin five years training for the Baptist Ministry.

I felt great!

2.

Baptist Ministry

'Holy Orders' is a 'one size fits all' kind of category, including what the RAF would class as C of E (Church of England), RC (Roman Catholic) and OD (Other Denominations). I think OD might also include Jews, Hindus, Buddhists and every other kind of religious affiliation. I suppose, 'Holy Orders' includes people of every sort whose vocation is defined by their religion. Perhaps the Commanding Officer, who appeared uncomfortable on this subject, is like most members of the general public who wonder what essential difference there is between people of different religious faiths. Since I am trying to plot my journey from being an Ordained Baptist Minister to becoming a Catholic layman, I need to give some defining features.

The difference between Anglican and Catholic churches is not as great as is often assumed. Theologians representing the two denominations meet from time to time, and their reports nearly always acknowledge 'areas of substantial agreement'. Anglican and Catholic churches are both institutional, that is to say, they have hierarchical governance with headquarter staff, respectively, Lambeth Palace in London and the Vatican in Rome. Both have primates, the Archbishop of Canterbury and the Pope. Both have bishops who resemble regional officers, with priests in local parishes who are answerable to their bishop. These churches are multi nationals, seeking State patronage and influence wherever they can find it.

Baptist churches are very different. Baptists are like independent traders, the congregations manage themselves. Baptists are dissenters who reject State interference and top-down religious structures. They reject a fixed liturgy and control by priests. Baptists cherish Christian Liberty and leave the responsibility to individual believers to decide for themselves matters such as birth control, divorce and abortion. Dissenters have strong theological, moral and political opinions, but they do not impose an obligation on members to support any official position. Baptists are proud advocates of religious tolerance, but this may have something to do with protecting themselves from persecution by Anglican and Catholic monarchs in the past; they have not always been zealous for freedom of conscience when they have been in the majority.

Differences between Protestant and Catholic Churches will be further discussed when issues arise in the following chapters. I am making these introductory remarks, to explain the peculiar way in which Baptist Ministers are appointed to their churches. As there is no hierarchy (although the Baptist Union has an Accredited List of Ministers who have been approved by a committee of ordained and lay representatives of local churches), the 'call to the pastorate' is a rather coy procedure in which Ministers seek churches, and churches seek Ministers!

Having completed my ministerial training and been admitted to the Accredited List as a Probationer, I was now free to seek a Church. In due course, I was approached by two churches, one in Wales and one in Southend-on-Sea. I went first to Wales to 'preach with a view', that is, I stayed for the weekend and preached at the Sunday morning and evening services at the Chapel. I now had to wait for the church members to vote.

The Secretary wrote to inform me that the members were most enthusiastic for me to become their new Minister. They would be enthusiastic: I was 25 years of age and married with a pretty wife! But the vote was not unanimous, a tiny minority expressed a preference for a Welshman. The Church in Southend-on-Sea was much smaller, situated on the dividing line between older, private houses, and a small Local Authority housing estate. The vote, on a second count, was unanimous. I had to decide. Mary and I tried to discern God's will, and in the end we decided to accept the invitation from the Southend church. At least I had the same accent!

I had hardly settled into my new church, when the local Probation Officer called. He told me that one of the streets in my area contained a higher proportion of young people on probation than any other street in Southend. He asked me what I intended to do for these anti-social youths? For the past five years my mind had been focussed on theology; I had not intended to do anything for unchurched people of any age group, unless it was to win them for Christ! This man was troubling me before my recent Ordination had time to fade from my memory. I told him I would think about it.

The congregation responded well to my leadership. They liked my suggestions for improving the appearance of the chapel and they agreed to some changes to the format of the services of worship. Nearly all the votes at church meetings were unanimous throughout the six years I was their Minister. They were a generous, hard working group of good people, with a few amusing characters to save us from monotony.

But what to do about the young people on the estate? These teenagers were not much younger than Mary and me. When the local newspaper reported a riot, which is supposed to have occurred when the Beatles gave a concert in the town, Mary and I knew the facts; we were in the audience at the time enjoying the show! Girls were screaming, and some were pushing their hair into their mouths, but that was fun. Some boys made a serious attempt to invade the stage, but the stewards protected the Stars. A girl in the space immediately before the stage fainted, which was the cue for many more girls to be overcome with hysteria, but that too was part of the fun.

Reflecting on the needs of young people, I realised that it is hard to escape a police record in our over regulated society, if you live on an estate, with few amenities and little money. We needed a youth club, but our church only had a space for worship. Thinking about this, I noticed a large raised area of concrete in the grounds of the church. Upon inspection, I realised this was the roof of a partly submerged public Air Raid Shelter, leftover from the war. Further investigation confirmed that the water could be pumped out and the broken furniture could be removed to provide a useful space. This could become a youth club. Once the church members approved, news of the venture spread quickly through the estate. It was only a few days before tradesmen living on the estate, offered their help to decorate and fit the place out as a youth club.

This was not a big project, quite small in scale, but it met a serious social need and was an immediate 'hit' with local young people. The members of the club were later to become the main body of volunteers in a surprising church initiative.

It all started with the church magazine. This was an ambitious publication, eight pages printed in two colours, containing not only church news, but articles of general interest. The magazine was distributed to every house in our neighbourhood. In one edition, I wrote an article, based on reports in *The Observer* and *The Guardian* newspapers, reporting the brutal suppression of an uprising of African people in the Portuguese Colony of Angola. There were reports of African terrorism, followed by reports of barbaric reprisals by the Portuguese. The Portuguese government was accused of being responsible for the massacre of tens of thousands of innocent Africans in Northern Angola. I included eye witness accounts which I obtained from Baptist Missionaries working in Angola.

My purpose in including general interest articles in the Church magazine was to show that Christians are interested in all aspects of life. The fact that the churches in Germany had largely remained silent during the persecution of Jews by the Nazi state, made Christians of my generation particularly aware that the

Church must speak out about abuses of power. Out of 165 African pastors and teachers in one part of Angola, 17 had been killed, 90 were 'disappeared', 30 were in prison, while only 28 were safe. These reports alone prompted concern among our Baptist community.

I showed my magazine article to two neighbouring Baptist ministers. The three of us decided to form an Angola Action Group, to campaign on behalf of Africans in Angola. My manse became the office from which the campaign was conducted. Every evening, young people from our church youth club, came to stuff envelopes with information and petitions, demanding that the British government withdrew their support for the Portuguese government's actions in Angola.

At a time when Britain was giving independence to its former colonies, Portugal claimed it was engaged in a 'civilising mission' in Africa. In response to international concerns, it was claimed that the uprising of Africans in Angola had been planned by Communists in Leopoldville, under the leadership of the Marxist, Roberto Holden. Roberto Holden was a Baptist Christian, opposed to Communism, who appealed for freedom for his countrymen on the basis of God's demand by Moses to Pharaoh, "Let my people go" (Exodus, chapter 5).

There were conflicting reports in the newspapers. Right-wing politicians, easily persuaded of Communist plots, and wanting to retain Britain's unique relationship with our 'oldest ally', agreed to arms supplies to Portugal and promised support at the United Nations Organisation. The Baptist Missionary Society, reluctantly at first, published first hand reports, not only of atrocities, but of iniquitous forced labour practices and physical punishments meted out to Africans who did not fulfil the demands of their employers.

Establishing the facts was difficult. After consulting my two colleagues in the Angola Action Group, and obtaining a loan for the purpose from my bank, I persuaded Mr George Thomas MP (later to become Speaker of the House of Commons) to accompany me on a fact-finding mission to the Congo-Angola border. When we returned, our press releases and photographic evidence were front page news in many newspapers. In September 1961, I was one of four Baptist ministers who was called to give evidence before the International Labour Organisation in Geneva (a part of the United Nations Organisation), in support of a complaint of forced labour in Angola.

It is not my purpose now to tell the story of the Angola Action Group and of the campaign to gain independence for Angola. I am simply giving this as an example of the prophetic mission of the Church, which is part of the Baptist tradition especially. It is precisely because Baptist churches keep apart from the State that they can more easily speak out on issues of social justice. The democratic structure of Baptist churches enable them to take political initiatives which are likely to be resisted by the hierarchies in other churches.

A letter to *The Observer* illustrates the difficulties the Roman Catholic Church has in criticising political policies of governments favourable to the Church. Written at the time of the struggle of the Africans for Angolan independence, and signed by two prominent Catholic laymen, the letter states:

"One of the more disturbing aspects of the Portuguese suppression of the rebellion in Angola is the indifference shown by many Roman Catholics in Britain to the increasing identification, however mistaken, of the Roman Catholic Church with the policies of the Portuguese administration. This is maintained in many ways, ranging from overt apologias for the Salazar regime to a general refusal to show concern for the brutal realities of the situation."

The penultimate paragraph in the letter reads:

"It is unfortunate that the Concordat of 1940, which reaffirms 'Portuguese spheres of influence' in which to 'christianise, to educate, to nationalise, and to civilise' is frequently interpreted as implying approval of Article 24 of the (Portuguese) Colonial Act of 1930, which states that 'Portuguese Catholic missions overseas, instruments of civilisation and national influence, shall have juridical personality and shall be protected and helped by the State as institutions of education."

Throughout the summer of 1961, *The Catholic Herald* gave prominence to articles by Hugh Kay defending Portuguese colonial policies and casting doubt on Gavin Young's reports in *The Observer* of Portuguese atrocities in Angola. If *The Catholic Herald* reflects the views of the Catholic Church, it confirms an impression that the Roman Catholic Church withholds support for liberation movements, while befriending right wing regimes.

Looking back over my first pastorate in Southend-on-Sea, I can see how my theology was developing since I became a Christian. When I became a Christian, I imagined the Kingdom of God being built up on a one to one basis, each convert in turn winning another, until at last the world is won for Christ! Such evangelistic zeal needs to be curbed. The Kingdom of God must always be optional. Totalitarian regimes, both political and religious, aim for world domination. Such ambition is always demonic. God in the Old Testament gave people the option between two ways (Jeremiah 21, 8). In the account of the Temptations of Jesus at the beginning of his earthly ministry, Jesus rejected the option of world domination (Matthew 4: 8-11).

The Reformation was largely about the Church trying to gain control of the State. The Catholic Church in the person of the Pope claimed God's authority over all the earth. King Henry VIII asserted the Divine Right of Kings. The Anglican Church sought to usurp the power of the Church of Rome. The Presbyterians attempted to subvert the Anglicans. The Dissenters demanded freedom of conscience. John Milton made a powerful case for Christian Liberty, although he drew the line when it came to tolerating Catholics! No wonder there is concern whenever it appears that the Church is becoming too much involved in politics.

During my first pastorate in Southend-on-Sea, I accepted that a consequence of freedom of conscience is that society will always be pluralistic. I was in transition from believing that the mission of the church is to win the world for Christ, towards believing that the mission of the church is to identify with the world as Christ did.

The role of the Church is not simply to fill gaps in public services, nor to propose political policies, but when the needs of neighbours are not being met, it is an obligation of the Gospel for a local church to consider if it is appropriate to take an initiative.

I welcome the emergence of the secular state. That people are emancipated from church control and look to the State for protection, surely fulfils a vision of the Kingdom of God when the distinction between secular and sacred will be lost (Revelation 21:22). It is inappropriate for the church to speak out on every social and moral issue, as if the Holy Spirit works only through the Church. Nevertheless, the Church still has a social function in demonstrating the Kingdom of God, and it still has a prophetic role in making the connection between sacral traditions and contemporary society.

During the last months in my first pastorate, I began reading the Baptist scholar Walter Rauschenbusch on the Social Gospel, and the Catholic priest Gustavo Gutierrez on Liberation Theology. These authors made clear that social action is an essential element of the Gospel. Following upon this reading, I attended a short study course at The William Temple College in Rugby. After this, I went to see the work of a Methodist Minister, Rev. Bill Gowland, who was making a serious attempt to relate the evangelical ministry of his local church to the industries in Luton.

It must have become apparent to my Baptist Area Superintendent that I was exploring the social implications of the Gospel. He approached me on behalf of the West Ham Central Mission about an appointment as an Industrial Chaplain. I said I would be interested and in due course I was appointed. With the co-operation of the Baptist Union and the Anglican Church, I later moved to the Anglican South London Industrial Mission. This was an exciting opportunity to work alongside an outstanding group of theologians, known as the South Bank Theologians, under Bishop Mervyn Stockwood and Bishop John Robinson. The next four years were to prove formative in my future ministry, with quite unforeseen consequences.

3

Reluctantly to Mass

My appointment as an Industrial Chaplain provided me with a modest stipend, but this was insufficient to secure a mortgage to buy a house for my wife, myself and three children. My wife, Mary, needed to return to teaching to give us a combined income sufficient to buy a property, which in turn required us to employ an au pair girl to look after our young children.

Elizabeth, our German au pair girl arrived by plane from Berlin. I met her at Heathrow Airport and we drove in my car to our newly acquired cottage in Essex. On the way, she said she hoped we would not mind that she was a Catholic, and added, "but I believe in the anti-baby pill!" This remark suggested she did not take her Catholic faith too seriously. But on the following Saturday evening, before going on her night out to the pub, she asked me where she could go on Sunday to Mass. This presented me with a real problem because there was no Catholic Church in our village, nor indeed nearby. I had no option but to drive her in my car at 7 a.m. on Sunday, to enable her to attend Mass at 8 a.m. Moreover, it was mid winter and the temperature was not much above freezing. When we arrived at the church, I elected to wait in the car while she fulfilled her religious obligation. My

Morgan car has a soft top, and by the time Elizabeth came out of the church, I was feeling almost frozen to death. When I complained, Elizabeth said sweetly, "Why did you not come with me into the Church?" I reminded her that I was a Protestant who objected to the Catholic Mass. She suggested I might object more strongly to staying outside in the cold!

During the following week, I visited the Catholic priest to explain my awkward position as a Baptist minister given the stark choice of attending Mass, or freezing to death. The priest said he would not object to my attending Mass provided I did not take Communion. The following Sunday I attended Mass for the first time.

It was not a lot warmer inside the Church than outside. I sat uncomfortably in the back pew, at six foot tall I was crammed into a pew made for a midget. I knew I would be expected to kneel for parts of the service, and I anticipated that this would be painful in the space available. This was worse than Economy Class in a budget airline.

The priest, having his back towards us, was bent over the altar, muttering words in Latin and doing things with a chalice and wafers. What had this to do with Jesus Christ? Prejudices which I suppose I inherited from generations of Protestant forbears, flooded my mind. I have no recollection of a sermon, but perhaps that is just as well!

The next Sunday was different. The priest explained with considerable regret, that the previous Sunday was the last time he was allowed to say Mass according to the rite he had been accustomed to since he was a child. This was the first Sunday for the new rite 'in the vernacular', that is, the liturgy was to be in English and the priest was to face the congregation. He said this was going to be a little strange, and he was as unsure as any of us as to how this would work out. Well, it worked out a lot better for me. The words and actions in the new liturgy were more intelligible.

The first part of the Mass consisted of readings from the Bible, which was reassuring to a Baptist. The priest used the occasion of the homily to explain the structure of the Mass which had been simplified in the new rite. The essential actions were: the offering of bread and wine, the blessing of the bread and wine, the breaking of the bread, and receiving the Body and Blood of Christ in Holy Communion. This series of actions was the same as that in commemorations of the Lord's Supper in Protestant churches. The prayers were spoken slowly and deliberately, perhaps the more so as both priest and congregation were not yet familiar with the new version. I felt more comfortable as a learner among learners. During the six months Elizabeth was with us as our au pair, I attended Mass every Sunday, albeit reluctantly at first.

I wonder what the Mass goers in that small Catholic Church speculated about the attendance of a girl in her late teens, who appeared to be a Catholic, and a man in his thirties, who appeared not to be? We roared into the church car park five minutes before Mass, and roared out again three minutes after the Mass. We hastened away to get home for breakfast prepared by Mary. After breakfast, our family drove ten miles to attend the 11 a.m. service at the Baptist church, returning home for lunch prepared by Elizabeth. The logistics worked, as long as the country roads were clear.

At about this time, I spent a night at a Bed and Breakfast establishment. The Guest House had an enormous assortment of old books. Typically, on one shelf there were a series of novels by Sir Walter Scott, *Lorna Doone, Pilgrim's Progress, Cruden's Concordance, The Admiralty Handbook of Wireless Technology Vol. I and Vol. II.* On another shelf, I discovered *The Shape of the Liturgy* by Gregory Dix. My attendance at Mass had aroused my interest in liturgy, so I took the book to bed with me. I skipped the more detailed academic passages and was thus able to get the gist of the essay in one sitting of about three hours.

Gregory Dix set out to describe the pattern of actions and words which formed the Eucharist since apostolic times. He emphasised the importance of the actions. Jesus had commanded his disciples to 'do' the Eucharist as a living act of worship: to take the bread and wine as Jesus had done (the Offertory), to bless the gifts as Jesus had done (the Eucharistic Prayer) to break the bread and give it to the disciples as an act of Holy Communion. This scholarly book clearly authenticated the actions of the Mass, although it did not attempt to deal with the important theological questions.

My theological education had begun during my five years as a student at the Bristol Baptist College and Bristol University. I enjoyed an academic study of the Old and New Testaments, and I accepted a critical approach to the text. This did not diminish my evangelistic zeal to win people for Christ. What happened in my first pastorate was that I no longer believed that my only interest in unbelievers was to convert them! I no longer regarded society as being more or less hostile to the Christian gospel, but rather I felt excitement in joining the whole human race in the struggle towards greater fulfilment, even though this meant sharing in the failures and the suffering.

I began to see worship in a new light. Sermons were not intended to bring unbelievers to a verdict of 'guilty' upon their lives, or as an invitation to accept Jesus as Saviour. Worship was for everyone to confess sin, and for all of us to discover the grace of Jesus Christ, the love of God, and inspiration of the Holy Spirit. I wanted to make this real. I began to see the Eucharist as a 'tangible' way for people to receive Jesus. This shifted the balance of worship from a 45 minutes sermon plus 15 minutes optional 'communion service', to a two part liturgy of Word and Sacrament, of roughly equal proportions.

My theological education was about to be continued further, and this included a deeper understanding of the Eucharist. My appointment to the South London Industrial Mission coincided with Bishop John Robinson becoming Chairman. It was about this time that John Robinson published his famous book, *Honest to God. The Guardian* newspaper described this book as, "probably the most talked about theological work of this century". Robinson judged that the time had come for a fundamental recasting of Christian Faith. The ensuing theological debate impinged upon the weekly chaplaincy team meetings.

The format for the weekly team meetings was: 8 a.m. Eucharist, followed by Bible study lead by Robinson, concluding with business items and reports from the Chaplains. The agenda frequently prompted vigorous theological discussion, providing a kind of crash course exploring the works of radical theologians such as Bonhoeffer, Buber, Bultman, Kierkegard and Tillich. Robinson's Bible study was based on St John's Gospel. I later discovered that this was the subject matter of his book, *The Priority of John*, which was published after his death in 1983.

It is assumed by many that Bishop John Robinson was a Liberal Protestant. In fact, Robinson saw clearly the inadequacy of Liberal theology. Some Liberals seemed to have reached the point of regarding Jesus as simply the best man who had ever lived. Robinson held to the New English Bible translation of John, chapter 1, verse 1: "what God was, the Word was." Robinson's comment on this verse is: "because Christ was utterly and completely 'the man for others', because he was love, he was 'one with the Father', because God is love". Far from stripping Jesus from his divinity, Robinson says, "at this point, of love 'to the uttermost', we encounter God" (page 76, *Honest to God*).

Robinson's devotion to the Eucharist can be seen in his book, *Liturgy Coming to Life*, which is his account of the Eucharistic liturgy at Clare College, Cambridge, when he was Dean from 1951–59. An extract from that book illustrates Robinson's intention to bring Christian worship 'down to earth' while at the same time bringing people into communion with God:

"From being merely symbols of the old order, they (the bread and the wine) become re valued as the vehicle, the body, of the living Christ. He redeems them from the world's use and releases them to perform their true function of carrying his own, eternal life to man" (pages 64–65).

In saying that in the Eucharist the bread and wine are 'revalued', Robinson seems to be suggesting transfiguration (the elements change their significance). However, in describing the bread and wine as "the vehicle, the body, of the living Christ . . . carrying his own, eternal life to man", Robinson is implying something akin to transubstantiation (the substance of the bread and wine change into the substance of the body and blood of Christ). Bearing in mind Robinson's intention of avoiding supernatural language, his description of what happens in the Eucharist, suggests that Christ changes bread from being food to sustain mortal life, into Christ's body bringing eternal life.

I think it would be fair to describe most of the Anglican Clergy belonging to the South London Industrial Mission as Anglo Catholics. For my part, I can say that they brought me to a deeper understanding of the Eucharist, and helped me to construct for myself a firm theological foundation for the next stage in my ministry.

4.

Called to Kingston

Bunyan Baptist Church was where I did not want to go. I had received a telephone call on the Friday evening asking me if I could preach there on Sunday because their Minister, Rev. Emlyn Nicholas, was ill. I had a terrible journey from my home in Essex to Kingston-upon-Thames, because it was Remembrance Sunday and it seemed that every town I had to pass through had Remembrance Day parades, closing roads to traffic. When at last I got to Kingston, I could see the Bunyan Baptist Church on my right, but the police were diverting traffic to the left, to allow the column of marchers to proceed to the town centre. Instead of arriving at the church on time, to enable the congregation to observe two minutes silence to remember the dead of two World Wars, I arrived late.

At the close of the service, Emlyn Nicholas, showing signs of terminal illness, made his way to the front to announce his resignation due to ill health. Then, suddenly revived, with a flourish he pointed to me and declared in a loud voice, "My successor is in the pulpit." I was indeed still in the pulpit, but I felt like replying with equal emphasis, "Oh no he isn't!"

Immediately afterwards, the Church Secretary hastened to apologise for their Minister's outburst. He gave the excuse that Emlyn was Welsh! I reassured him that I enjoyed being an Industrial Chaplain and was not ready to return to a pastorate.

The Church members subsequently expressed an interest in pursuing their former Minister's suggestion that I should be considered for their now vacant pastorate. A strongly worded letter from the Area Superintendent warned them off considering me. In the meantime, I had been head hunted for an interesting position in Warwick. Eventually, I was invited to become the Minister of the Bunyan Baptist Church, and after dealing with my sense of foreboding, I accepted the invitation.

Let me explain my reservations about going to Kingston. In the first place, I did not want to live in a London suburb, especially in an affluent borough like Kingston-upon-Thames. Even the name of the place is pretentious, The Royal Borough of Kingston-Upon-Thames. The suffix 'upon' is class conscious, nearly every other town on a river uses 'on'. But Kingston, don't you know, was where the Saxon Kings of England used to be crowned? I am from the other side of the river, as my accent, half cockney and half Essex, shows. Kingston Hill is home to some of the richest people in the UK, it is situated where the Thames runs through grassy banks, it has Bushy Park and Richmond Park at its heart, and Hampton Court Palace is only a mile away. This is not where I wanted to be. What is more relevant, as I was to discover, Kingston represented the kind of society which many young people in the nineteen sixties were rebelling against. I would soon find out the nature and strength of that rebellion.

The old Bunyan Baptist Chapel, built in 1867, represented features of Calvinism which I dislike. Baptists trace their origins back to Calvin and Zwingli. Calvin was founder of the most radical branch of Protestantism. He taught that God has predestined some people to salvation (the Elect) and others to damnation. He believed that the Elect are recognisable. They eschew all forms of pleasure and frivolity. Baptists of my generation did not dance, sing popular songs, go to the cinema, gamble, drink alcohol, smoke or swear. They were strict in Sunday Observance and churchgoing. They dressed in a manner suggesting sober life styles with a hint of savings in the bank.

The architecture of the old Bunyan Chapel was Victorian, not like an Anglican or Catholic Church, distinctly a Nonconformist Chapel. The large Rose window and fine oak doors at the front of the building, indicated that the members of this congregation had worked and saved hard. Inside, the organ pipes reached across almost the entire width of the seven hundred seat auditorium. The pulpit large enough for two or three preachers, and twelve foot high, was centre stage leaving no one in any doubt that preaching was the main function of worship. The Communion Table was modest, not immediately obvious at the foot of the pulpit. The Baptistry was not even visible, under the floorboards, opened up whenever a person, recently saved, was immersed in water prior to being received into the membership of the Church.

At the beginning of the Bunyan Baptist Church, the members had asserted their commitment to Calvinism. This may have been a reaction against shallow evangelism which uses emotional manipulation to get people to make 'a decision for Christ'. Calvin put the emphasis upon God's action in salvation, and played down human decision. Some evangelists call upon people to make a decision for Christ and to witness to their faith in baptism.

The emphasis is upon the human decision and the human witness, not upon the grace of God and the action of the Holy Spirit. The members of the Bunyan Church made clear by their commitment to Calvinism, that they rejected evangelistic campaigns of this sort. Salvation is only possible through God's grace and power. Calvinism, taken to extreme, overlooks the necessity of human co-operation in salvation. It can also lead to preaching to the converted (i.e. the Elect) without any concern for the world since the vast majority of people, according to this doctrine, are predestined to hell anyway! This is the opposite to the gospel I preach, which sees the struggle of humanity as being the passionate concern of God and the main focus for the mission of the Church.

Jesus proclaimed the Kingdom of God, which is the realisation of God's purpose for the whole of creation. The Church was never intended to be a recruiting agent for God; it is meant to go out from its communion with God into the world to impregnate society with godliness, always respecting people's freedom to reject God, until and unless they find their fulfilment in him. Ultimately, the hope is that there will be no need for a temple because the world will have become fully incorporated into God. But this must remain a hope, because no person's co-operation must be assumed, or forced. The Church must identify itself with the human struggle, even lose itself in service to the world.

At the outset of my ministry in Kingston, I was determined to do something about the dreariness of the Sunday services of worship. The Baptist Renewal Group, of which I was a founder member, had for a number of years proposed the need for a renewal of worship in Baptist churches, but there was no evidence of such renewal in this congregation which, as the architecture made clear, was still dominated by preaching, with hymns being the only items of congregational participation. Worse still, the Lord's Supper was only celebrated once a month, with holy communion being seen as an optional extra.

During the first two years at Bunyan, I regularly preached on different aspects of the Eucharist. I pointed my congregation to those passages in the New Testament which indicated that the early church celebrated the Lord's Supper weekly, or even daily in house meetings. I quoted from documents of the early church showing that Sunday worship followed a pattern of readings from scripture, followed by a sermon, and prayers, after which bread and wine were offered, blessed, broken and given to the faithful. That this order was preserved by the Reformers is seen in this quotation from Calvin: "Thus it became the unvarying rule that no meeting of the church should take place without the Word, prayers, partaking of the Supper, and almsgiving. That this was the established order among the Corinthians also, we can sufficiently infer from Paul" (1 Corinthians 11:20).

After careful study and lengthy discussion at church members meetings over a period of two years, this pattern of weekly Eucharistic worship was gradually introduced.

As to the meaning of the eucharist, there has been a renewal of sacramental theology among Baptists in recent times. The concept of 'transignification' was helpful in bringing members of the Bunyan Church to a fuller understanding of the sacrament. In becoming a Catholic, I have not had to revise my understanding of the mystery of the bread and wine becoming the body and blood of Christ by the Holy Spirit, which has been my belief most of my years as a Christian.

Previous generations of ministers of the Bunyan Baptist Church had a reputation for Expository preaching. The preacher would go through a passage of scripture, verse by verse, finding the truth contained in the text. The situation is different today. Christians are bombarded by expert sceptical opinion which leads many young people to be in doubt about the faith handed on to them from previous generations. Even older Christians sometimes lack confidence in their ability to give adequate reasons for the faith they hold. It is the urgent task of a preacher to give careful thought to the appointed scripture, or the appointed feast, and ask, how can I make sense of this item of Christian faith, being aware of the mindset of people today?

At the same time as renewing the worship and reconsidering our mission, the members of the church needed to discern what service was needed in our neighbourhood. Jesus demonstrated the Kingdom of

God in a series of miracles, or as the fourth gospel prefers, signs. The first of these signs was turning water into wine at a marriage feast. What exactly happened we shall never know, but Jesus demonstrated that human resources can be stretched in an exceptional manner, to meet human need. As a local church, we needed to discern if there was need in our neighbourhood which we could meet, with the help of God.

The miracle highlighted by all the gospel writers is 'The Feeding of the Multitude' (Matthew 14:13-21; Mark 8:1-10; Luke 9:12-17; John 6:1-14). This demonstration of the Kingdom of God, showed people coming together, sharing inadequate resources, and with the inspiration and power of the Holy Spirit, meeting the needs of five thousand people; and the Kingdom of God became a reality. The question for our church members was this: In what ways might we demonstrate the Kingdom of God in our neighbourhood? This sounds vague, and it was vague, until we found what it was God wanted us to do. Then, it became all too real!

5.

Kaleidoscope

Searching for clues to discover the future mission of the John Bunyan Baptist Church to its local community, I bought copies of the local newspapers: *The Surrey Comet* and *The Borough News*. Both papers took as their main story, the alarming situation on a Friday night in the area around Kingston railway station. The station is a few hundred yards from the site of the church. According to the newspapers, I was about to encounter a scene of drug induced violence beyond the control of the police, resulting in serious injuries and deaths from drug overdose. Could this really be true?

On the next Friday night, Mary and I ventured down town to where the action was alleged to take place. At 9 p.m. the town was surprisingly quiet, except for the steady flow of traffic moving in the direction of Central London. As we approached the Three Fishes public house, adjacent to the railway station, we could hear the throb of loud music. We tried to enter, but the press of bodies, the loudness of the music, and the dense cigarette smoke made this difficult. Since it had been our purpose to discover what was happening, we determinedly squeezed into the darkened interior, and made out the shapes of people moving in time to the music. Many seemed to be in some kind of hypnotic trance. Until then I had not smelt cannabis, but I guessed the herbal scent I detected was the forbidden weed. This was it, the scene that the newspapers complained about, but there was no hint of violence, rather peaceful in fact.

At 10.30 p.m. the barman rang the bell and shouted the traditional, "Time gentlemen please!" Everyone moved towards the exit. Outside, we were met by a crowd of youths coming from the Kingston Hotel, on the opposite side of the road. The people we were with from the Three Fishes wore their hair long, the girls were in long dresses, the boys in torn jeans and sandals. A crowd coming towards us looked menacing, they were skinheads, familiar to me from my time in East London. It was not their shaved heads which struck fear in us, but their heavy boots and the barely concealed weapons under their jackets. Almost instantly fighting broke out. The skinheads were out numbered ten to one, but they were equipped to fight and fuelled by alcohol and amphetamines. The hippies did not want to fight, but when one was seen to have blood streaming from his face, they had no option but to defend themselves as best they could. Police arrived to separate the combatants and keep the road clear for traffic. The Rockers arrived from The Swan public house in uniforms of long jackets on boys and wide skirts on girls, both sexes wearing dancing shoes. When the Mods came in, on their multi mirrored scooters, more fighting broke out. Police vehicles with flashing blue lights and screaming sirens added to the confusion, then an ambulance arrived to take the first casualty to hospital. Welcome to Kingston-upon-Thames in the year 1967.

For the predominately middle class residents in the Royal Borough of Kingston-upon-Thames, the behaviour of a section of young people in their town was downright disgraceful. Parents expected young people to enjoy themselves. The older generation recalled their own enjoyment at the weekly Dance, in the village hall maybe in pre-war days, or held on camp during their time in the Forces. In their day, young men asked girls who sat waiting to be invited to dance fox-trots and waltzes that permitted closeness within limits. Elvis Presley broke this pattern with his pulsating rhythms and uninhibited movement. The Beatles looked smart, but the hidden messages in their performances prompted girls to break through police lines, rush the stage and do almost anything and everything to touch their idols, and if this was not possible, they screamed and fainted in hysteria. The Rolling Stones were an even greater threat to decency, law and order; their message was not only sexual freedom, it also carried a political overtone. But there was something else. When the Rolling Stones made their emphatic cry that they could 'get no satisfaction', it was in despair of post war British society and a yearning for a more meaningful human existence. All this was intolerable to upright citizens who demanded action by the police.

The BBC at this time, reflecting middle class anxieties, refused to broadcast most of this music. The rebellion was driven underground but surfaced in places like Eel Pie Island near to Kingston, and in The

Three Fishes public house in the centre of Kingston. The Rolling Stones began playing at the Station Hotel, in Richmond, the next borough to Kingston. The members of the alternative society gathered at their chosen venues; the boys put on their torn jeans, the girls put on grandmother's wedding dress or gowns bought from old stock in second hand shops. Carnaby Street and other less well known retail outlets gladly supplied exotic fashions to meet the growing demands from the street. In secret these young people passed round cannabis reefers, and some paid for more dangerous drugs. But mixed with this sedition, there was a powerful longing for something new and better. Donovan, the Hurdy Gurdy Man, who some claim was a founder of 'Flower Power' in Britain, issued his top selling record, *Catch The Wind*. It is a song about young love, but the title refers also to a hopeful mood which prevailed among the devotees of the music scene of the 60's. So, while respectable citizens protested, clergymen condemned, and doctors warned of spinal injuries due to extreme dancing and birth defects attributable to cannabis use, I determined to explore this youth scene to discover the spiritual content which I was sure was present. That was why I urged the members of the John Bunyan Baptist Church to invite the late night crowd on to our church premises on Friday nights after the pubs closed.

The members of the John Bunyan Baptist Church were not easily persuaded. None of the members had thought of a mission as challenging as this. There were good reasons for us to turn our attention to other matters of urgent concern: we had a declining membership, our finances were critical, our buildings in need of repair, our membership was ageing. At the same time, we were in the process of renewal of our Sunday services of worship, could we really take on board the problems of our borough?

After much anxious deliberation and prayerful discernment, it was resolved to develop our church premises to serve the needs of the people we had identified in our immediate locality. The decision by the church members was to prove momentous. At this stage, all I asked for was permission to adapt a large church hall to provide a club, open from 10 p.m. on Fridays to 6 a.m. on Saturdays.

With the help of a few volunteers, we painted one wall of the club black, with illuminated coloured cut outs to create a pattern like a Kaleidoscope. The idea was that people with different life styles can come together to become a beautiful community. We built a counter for food and purchased a Gaggia for making coffee. A record deck and Hi Fi loud speakers were installed. The skilled job of playing the right discs was to be entrusted to John and Rob Christmas, twin teen-age members of our church who knew the music scene.

The Club was not an instant success. One night, a Canadian girl, Jan Johnston, came to the Club and listened to my explanation of our intentions. She invited me back to her squat (a house without legal tenancy) and introduced me to her companions, David and Andrea. During the following week, at their request, I introduced them to my understanding of Christian faith and broke bread with them in the manner of a Eucharist. Jan then took charge of changing the décor of the Club, and suggested a vegetarian menu. Richard was seeking somewhere to live after coming down from Cambridge University, and he introduced some other friends from University. Soon we had 'a commune' of about a dozen volunteers, who lived in our former caretaker's house, and were the staff group for the Club which suddenly became popular with the late night crowd in Kingston.

During the early years of operation, the Club was often disrupted by a group of Hell's Angels. Allegations of drug dealing on the premises triggered police raids. Gradually as the Club became increasingly valued by the people attending, the situation improved and a strong sense of loyalty developed. Most nights passed without serious incident, indeed the atmosphere was usually joyful and peaceful. People outside assumed that the Club pulsated with loud music, but more often than not, the sounds were subtle, or when recordings of the Incredible String Band were played, it could even be described as ethereal.

One night a girl collapsed in the club. My first thought was to call an ambulance, but her companions insisted she would quickly recover, given a glass of water. I was relieved that the girl did quickly regain consciousness, but I was far from satisfied that she was all right. I decided to call a doctor known to me. He examined the girl in an adjoining room and told me of his concerns. The girl was pregnant, she was malnourished, she had bronchitis, she was a drug addict and homeless. The doctor explained the difficulties in such cases. She needed to attend ante natal clinic, chest clinic, drug clinic to name the obvious;

being homeless it would prove impossible to make appointments. He expressed dismay at cases such as this. That is when I had a good idea: perhaps the doctor could attend Friday night sessions and run a clinic in the room adjoining the club. He did not share my enthusiasm and his wife vetoed the proposal. With perseverance however, I persuaded a philanthropist to put up the money to establish the clinic staffed by a doctor and a nurse. That is how our medical service started.

Jan and the other commune members offered to take the homeless girl into their house. This was the first of many vulnerable people they took in. The old house was not fit for purpose, and a visit by the Council's Environmental Health Officer gave the threat of a closure order. I had made friends with the Borough Youth Officer and with the Director of Social Services. When the matter of a closure order on the house came up for decision by the Council, the Director of Social Services and the Youth Officer pleaded for a grant to pay for essential repairs, and in addition they proposed a grant from the Youth Service budget for our work with 'hard to reach' young people in the Borough.

Although the decision by the Council to make a grant to Kaleidoscope indicated a degree of confidence in the social value of the project, the description of the people who came to the club as 'hard to reach', recognised that a section of the population was in rebellion against mainstream society. One Councillor, knowing the alienation many young people felt, declared that he would not be surprised if Kaleidoscope would refuse help from the Council.

Those who suspected that there was a radical edge to Kaleidoscope, were right: the club was more than a place to enjoy music deemed inappropriate by the BBC, it was a meeting place for many who felt estranged from the established order. These young people were not attracted to mainstream political parties, nor to churches of any denomination, nor did they want to be at home with their parents. They were anti-war because they did not feel inclined to defend Western style democracy. They had utopian ideas of non-judgemental, non possessive, equal relationships, which if not a realistic possibility in the present society, could hopefully be experienced in psychedelic festivals, or in the Kaleidoscope club of the John Bunyan Baptist Church on Friday nights!

People who believe religion is a form of escapism, will see in the unrealistic aspirations of the 60's youth rebellion something akin to religion. All religions predicate a degree of detachment from this world, and all religions invite people to discover a spiritual state of perfect peace. For my part, I saw in that generation's rebellion a frustrated quest for the Kingdom of God. Kaleidoscope was meant to be a demonstration of what that kingdom might be like. The vegetarian food, the good coffee, the hospitality, the acceptance of every kind and condition of person, the doctor and the nurse bringing healing, the church minister bringing forgiveness, the staff being the people of God clearing up the mess and facilitating the communion: this was a demonstration of a theological vision.

Rock music owes much to its Gospel origins, but this is not the extent of the spiritual content in the music of the 60's and 70's. Donovan, as he stood on the seashore, with the lovely girl at his side, her hand resting in his, hoped he might 'catch the wind'. Later on, when he realised that sex was not the highest expression of life, he was introduced by George Harrison to the teaching of the Maharishi Yogi. Cross-legged on the Persian carpet, the incense curling up into the air, Donovan and George turned their thoughts to the East and to an ashram by the Ganges river. Was it enlightenment, or the fair-haired Jenny Boyd he sought? It was not clear, but his spiritual search was sincere, as was that of many of the Stars of the 60's and 70's. Christian theologians still debate whether in Hinduism and Buddhism there are paths to God, but for me there is no doubt that the Wind of the Holy Spirit, the third person of the Holy Trinity, is active in other religions. For me, Jesus is the Word of God, the Light of the World who enlightens everyone (John 1; 1 to 9).

Many of the Stars of that time travelling from the West to the East found their journeys ended in disillusion. Jesus taught that commitment and faithfulness are required if we are to enter the Kingdom of God. John Bunyan, in his 17th century classic *Pilgrims Progress*, told of the many temptations and wrong paths which divert all but the most determined pilgrims from reaching the Celestial City. Repentance and rebirth are pre-requisites of salvation. Sitting cross-legged on a Persian carpet, with or without incense, is not the most promising start!

Although a start had been made to reach out to the young people in our down town location, not much else would seem to have changed in the life of the John Bunyan Baptist Church. Built by Victorians, the Baptist chapel I inherited gave every appearance of being a relic of the past. At the beginning of my ministry in Kingston, people arriving for Sunday worship could expect the usual Baptist order of service: four hymns, long prayers, readings from the Bible and a substantial 30 minutes sermon. A close observer, however, would have noticed that as some of the older members of the church left or died, a new group of young people, most of them recently from university, joined the congregation.

This group of young adults attending our services wanted radical change, not only in society, but in the church also. There was a positive response to my theology which had developed during my association with Bishop John Robinson at the South London Industrial Mission, and there was a growing desire to see some of this theology taking shape in the worship and mission of our church. After two years of questioning and prayerful discernment by the church members in monthly meetings, it was resolved to demolish the existing church buildings, and re-develop the site to provide new buildings to facilitate a renewal of our worship and our new commitment to social action. It is not my purpose now to describe the mundane struggles in re-developing the site, sufficient to say that the new buildings were officially opened in 1977 by Mr George Thomas MP, later to become Speaker of the House of Commons, and Rev. Dr Ernest Payne, Vice President of the Baptist Union, and a President of the World Council of Churches.

The new chapel is an irregular eight-sided shape, which allows the congregation on four sides to face a central communion table. The cruciform shape of the concrete ceiling, and an overhead circle of candles, emphasises the central place of the Eucharist in the church's life. A baptistry, large enough for an adult to be immersed, is a prominent feature. The lectern provides for preaching the Word of God. The organ assists the congregation in hymn singing.

It was not chiefly the architecture of the new chapel which changed the worship, it was people coming into the church from outside the Baptist denomination who made the greatest difference. When our church opened its doors to outsiders, it thought it was giving to our local community; but we received from the Kaleidoscope project far more than we gave. (Jesus said, "Those who lose their life for my sake, and for the sake of the gospel, will save it", Mark 8:35.)

Sally Murray was a resident in nearby Surbiton, who came as a volunteer to work at Kaleidoscope. Learning that the John Bunyan church had 'open membership' (people who are Christians, but not Baptists, can become members), Sally was the first Roman Catholic to become a member of our church. George Short was an Anglo Catholic who came to work at Kaleidoscope. Having been an Organ Scholar at Lampeter, he became our church organist and nudged me towards adopting the Church Calendar. Richard Fitzsimmonds came from traditional Baptist stock, he made the church furniture, and later made the transition to Catholicism before me. Gabrielle Ayerst had since early years felt a vocation to the priesthood.

Gabrielle came to work at Kaleidoscope, introduced us to many features of Catholic worship, including Stations of the Cross and Benediction; she was elected a deacon and given permission on occasions to sing the Eucharistic Prayer. She married John, and has since become an ordained Anglican priest. Myfanwy Franks, and her daughter Non, are Roman Catholics. Myfanwy is an artist who worked at Kaleidoscope. She made an icon of Jesus on the cross, an icon of the Virgin Mary, and painted a large canvas illustrating the Resurrection; all of which were hung on the walls of the chapel. These are a few of the people who influenced our worship and helped me on my spiritual journey.

Because the church had developed its service to the local community, its worship reflected the community's different denominational traditions. More significantly, the church congregation included people of different religious backgrounds. In his 1977 presidential address to the Baptist Union, Dr Ernest Payne referred to the John Bunyan Baptist Church in Kingston as an ecumenical experiment "which should give us satisfaction".

In the new chapel, the order of service was based upon descriptions of Sunday worship in documents from the first and second centuries of the Christian Church, and showed awareness also of modern developments in the Church of England and the Roman Catholic Church. This order of service brings together the preaching of the Word of God and the Breaking of Bread. This is the order of service:

PART ONE – LITURGY OF THE WORD

Member: We are here in the name of Jesus Christ

President: Jesus said: Where two or three are gathered together in my name, I am there among them.

Our Lord taught us that we should freely confess our faults and forgive the faults of others, therefore let us call to mind our sins.

President: Lord have mercy

People: Lord have mercy

President: Christ have mercy

People: Christ have mercy

President: We confess to Almighty God and to each other, that we have sinned through our own fault, and that in our life together we have often failed to be the Body of Christ in the world.

People: Almighty God, have mercy on us, forgive us our sins, and bring us to everlasting life.

President: In the name of Christ, Amen.

THE GLORIA

READING from the Old Testament or Epistles

PSALM or hymn based on a psalm

INTERCESSIONS

GOSPEL READING

SERMON

HYMN

PART TWO – THE BREAKING OF BREAD

OFFERING

HYMN

President: Lift up your hearts

People: We lift them up unto the Lord

President: Let us give thanks to the Lord our God

People: We join in the eternal hymn of praise

President: We join Mary, the apostles, those who have gone before us in the faith, and all God's people saying:

People: Holy, holy, holy Lord,
God of power and might,
Heaven and earth are full of your glory,
Hosanna in the highest.
Blessed is he who comes in the name of the Lord. Hosanna in the highest.

THANKSGIVING PRAYER
concluding with Lord's Prayer.

BREAKING OF BREAD

HOLY COMMUNION

DOXOLOGY

BLESSING

DISMISSAL

Visitors from other Baptist churches usually express pleasure at experiencing what is new to them, and Anglicans and Catholics who visit, say they feel 'at home' with the liturgy. The theology in the prayer of thanksgiving is recognisable by Catholics, who express their surprise that some Protestants believe in the Real Presence of Christ in the sacrament. Although there is no uniformity of belief, no Protestant believes in the Real Absence! It is hard to assess such matters, but I believe that the radical changes in our worship greatly strengthened our devotion to Jesus Christ and invigorated our service to the community outside of the church.

The new Kaleidoscope club was built underneath the chapel, at basement level. That the club was located directly beneath the sanctuary, that the record studio was underneath the baptistry, and that the red AGA cooker enabled us to celebrate something akin to the Eucharist: these signified that worship and community belong together. I doubt if many who came to the club were conscious of this significance, but on many occasions people told me that the club was for them a sacred place. Wherever people are gathered together in communion with one another, there Christ is present, even if he is not named.

In the new basement club, there were occasional incidents of violence that reminded us that we still needed to be delivered from evil, but it became more and more evident that Kaleidoscope was dispensing a healing warmth into the community. We had achieved an 'outreach' to many people who felt isolated and excluded, many who were angry, and many whose hope for a 'new age' was without any solid foundation. We were not wanting to re-adapt rebels back into society, we wanted to help bring about a better society where everyone could thrive.

A surgery, staffed by a doctor and two nurses, was situated to the side of the club. This gave immediate access to treatment for anyone coming off the street into the club, on a Friday night. This provided confidential help to drug users, first aid to people injured in a fight, and a first doctor's appointment for any girl who was pregnant. Later, this service expanded into day care and residential drug rehabilitation.

Two-thirds of the church site was re-developed, providing hostel accommodation for young people who could not live at home and needed the residential care provided by the Kaleidoscope staff.

One Friday night, a fragile old man came down the steps into the club. He accepted a helping hand and sat heavily on the chair I pushed under him. His body appeared to be kept in place by his collarless white shirt underneath a black serge suit which fitted him tightly. He had clearly seen better days, and it seemed equally clear he was unlikely to see many more. I offered him tea or coffee. He said he preferred coffee. He had a cultured voice, perhaps he had been a High

Court Judge, or the Conductor of an orchestra? What was he doing here?

After drinking his coffee, he asked me if I was the person in charge. I said I was. He seemed displeased as he told me he had heard that I was a Baptist Minister. When I confirmed this fact he said, "I am sorry about that. Baptists always want to convert people. You must not try to convert these people," and looking around with great compassion he declared, "they are beautiful as they are!"

After about an hour, he indicated that he wanted to go. He needed help to get out to the pavement, but he was adamant that he could find his way home. A few days later, I heard that he had been found dead. He had been identified as a former Vice Principal of Wells Theological College.

I believe this former Anglican clergyman had a deliberate purpose in visiting the Kaleidoscope that night. He was unlikely simply to have been passing by, he had discovered that the person in charge was a Baptist, and having delivered his message he went home. It was as if, reviewing his life as a priest, he had come to the conclusion that the Church is often wrong in its understanding of unbelievers, especially those with an unconventional life style. He came to Kaleidoscope to see for himself that people are beautiful, the poorer sort, the more so!

This member of a theological college must have struggled with traditional doctrines of sin for him to have come, at the end of his life to a bright vision of the human condition. Protestant theology during the 20th century was dominated by Karl Barth who contrasted the holiness of God and the sinfulness of man to such an extent that it was difficult to see anything of God in man. There is abundant evidence to support a pessimistic theology; but that is not the conclusion that priest came to, neither is it my conclusion.

Reflecting further on what the elderly clergyman said, I identified a significant difference between my own theology and that of many Baptists. Baptists reject infant baptism, and believe that a person in order to be saved must acknowledge their sins, repent and accept the salvation offered through Jesus Christ. This explains why some Baptists, as well as being concerned for the person, have another agenda when they provide social services. Believing that a person is alienated from God, "dead in trespasses and sins" (Ephesians 2:1), until and unless a person comes to faith in Christ, they feel an obligation to confront people with the gospel. Most Christians accept infant baptism, therefore many people will be offended by the suggestion that they are not 'saved' if they have not experienced ' a conversion moment'.

Most Catholics are 'cradle Catholics', that is to say, they were born into a Catholic family and therefore part of the 'household of faith' (Acts 16:15; 1 Corinthians 1:16). In order to free them from original sin, the baby needs to be baptised shortly after birth. For Catholics, conversion is a continuous process. Beginning before birth through the abundant grace of God and the faith of parents (or sponsors), the infant becomes a full member of the Church at Baptism, they join the procession to the altar for blessing at Holy Communion, they are taught the faith and prepared for their First Communion at about the age of 7, they make their own adult profession of faith and commitment at their Confirmation at about the age of 12, and they continue thereafter to grow in faith through regular participation in the Eucharist.

I believe that Christ died for all, and that the Holy Spirit offers to all the possibility of salvation. "He is the sacrifice that takes our sins away, and not only ours, but the whole world's." (1 John 2:1-5). The gift of freedom gives to everyone personal responsibility for their decisions and actions. Just as evil can be found in this life, by extension I can imagine hell as a condition of alienation from God in the future life; but I find it impossible to believe God punishes people in hell because they were ignorant of the gospel, or neglectful of baptism. Putting aside considerations of church dogma, in practice I see we are all on a 'continuum', at one end there is a state of almost total alienation from God, at the other end there is a state of almost complete Christhood; we are all on that continuum, some moving forward, some moving backward: hopefully God will bring us to salvation in the future life. Jesus in his earthly ministry identified some people who, while being outside the perimeters of organised religion, were accepted by God, while some others, who were outwardly religious, were rejected (Matthew 25: 31-46).

In my relationship with the Road Rats (a breakaway group of Hells Angels) I can see a continuous growth in trust and mutual respect. In my book *No Quick Fix* I described the terror and carnage we experienced in

Kaleidoscope when Road Rats first visited the club. Over a period of five years, that hostility changed as we began to understand each other. One of the Rats put it like this to me, "We were the boys at the back of the class, who were sent out of the class, and eventually excluded from the school. Academic subjects were simply not our thing. We were bored to the point of becoming disruptive". He earned his living landscaping gardens. Another was a plumber. Another was a bricklayer. Another found satisfying work at a garage specialising in high performance cars. None was unemployed. They had courage, they had discipline among themselves, and they had a sense of honour. What they were rebelling against was the assumption in our present society that respect should be shown only to clever people, the so-called entrepreneurs, " people who con the rest of us into giving them wealth and honours, while they think of new ways of cutting costs and squeezing ever more profit out of the hard working poor". The Rats are angry, and each of them has a story to tell explaining why.

The surprising thing about my relationship with the Road Rats is that in the end they trusted me to be a priest among them. On the first occasion, they sent for me when Becky died. Becky was a free spirit and centre of attraction at any party. To the Road Rats, she was their girl. She died of an overdose of drugs. They asked me to conduct the funeral. Dozens of their associates attended, and afterwards at the cemetery they threw flowers into the grave before filling in the earth. They made a similar call to me when two of their number were shot in a fight. On that occasion, hundreds of Hells Angels and other biker groups attended. On another occasion, I conducted a wedding ceremony for them at a remote outcrop of rock in Cornwall.

This relationship with the Road Rats meant that after a long period when they had cast an evil shadow over the club, they became our defenders. One girl said to me, "I always feel safe when the Road Rats are in the club". It was true, they ensured the club was a place of safety. I have come to believe that many people need the mediating role of a priest. Being unsure of their condition before God, many people desperately need to be told, on the authority of Christ and his Church, that they are accepted and forgiven. I have not been persuaded that the ordained priest should always and only be a celibate male.

There is, in addition to the particular ministry of the ordained priest, a priesthood of all believers. When we gather together to celebrate the Eucharist, we proclaim the sacrifice Christ offered once for all on the cross, so that by the power of the Holy Spirit, the sacrifice of the cross is made present for us. In the Eucharist we unite ourselves to Christ in his intercession to the Father on behalf of all people. We pray not only for ourselves, but that the Eucharistic sacrifice may advance the peace and salvation of all the world.

Kaleidoscope was never intended to be simply a service provider. When Mary and I came to Kingston, we discovered a crowd of young people on the doorstep of our church who were alienated from post war society; the world of their parents was not the world they wanted to inhabit. We shared a vision with members of our church to provide hospitality to this downtown community. In their company we caught a wind of change, we thought perhaps it was a wind of the Holy Spirit; a dissatisfaction with things as they were, a longing for a more authentic lifestyle. In the deepest sense, these young people were homeless. Kaleidoscope was meant to be a space for people who were exploring their own feelings and needs, and seeking a new direction. The core group, 'the commune' or 'the staff', worked hard to provide appropriate medical treatment, care and support. But these are only the bare necessities; Kaleidoscope provides the space, the warmth, the hospitality, that we all need to enable us to thrive.

Perhaps what Kaleidoscope was trying to be, was in essence what a church should be. I certainly saw Kaleidoscope as a celebration of life. We enjoyed many festive occasions: 'Ebenezer Suppers' (a weekly vegetarian meal for those living in squats); hot cross buns on Good Friday; mince pies in the Friday night club at Christmas; Christmas Day dinner (on this occasion turkey was served, followed by Christmas pudding flambéed in brandy). In January, we rehearsed and performed pantomime, attended by church members, hostel residents, residents from a nearby old people's home, together with the Road Rats, their wives, girl friends, and children. Every Sunday, lunch was served in the club, attended by single members of the church and hostel residents. Every weekday, lunch was served in the club for local business people, teachers from two local schools and other members of the public.

Kaleidoscope was fully inclusive, and the AGA cooker was 'on' day and night, every day and every night! This was truly a church; and the Eucharist was celebrated daily because Word and Sacrament were the hidden heart of it all.

6.

Invitation from the Apostolic Delegate

The local Baptist Ministers' Fraternal was a predictable affair in the 1970's. We met once a month in one of the churches in the Kingston and Richmond area. Men, they were all men at that time, started to arrive at 9.45 a.m. for 10 a.m. After the usual banter, references to sporting events, so and so's new car, jokes about Ron who appears to win converts every Sunday, or Ted who says he loses members every week, the minister who was our host for the day welcomed us to his church and opened the meeting with prayer. One of our number would then give a paper on a biblical, theological or social topic. This was followed by a discussion; the majority who were Evangelical Conservatives disagreeing with the minority who were Liberals. At mid day we adjourned for lunch, which had been prepared for us by the 'Ladies' of the host church. At the end of the repast, we called the 'Ladies' into the room to thank them for the splendid spread. All this was predictable.

What was utterly unpredictable was an invitation, read out to us by the Secretary, from the Apostolic Delegate from the Vatican, for one of us to go to the Delegate's nunciature at nearby Wimbledon, to give a Baptist response to the Pope's encyclical *Humanae*

Vitae. Rev. Herbert, whose face always flushed red at the mention of Rome, the Pope, or Catholicism, was outraged. He declared that this was a Jesuit plot. Others, less extreme in their Protestantism, felt that perhaps one of us should go as a gesture of good will, although it was unlikely we would have anything in common except opposition to abortion.

Rev. Herbert felt that the time had come, he could hesitate no longer, he would be frank about it: he had heard from his barber when he went for a haircut, that a local Baptist minister was in the habit of attending the 8 a.m. Mass on Sundays at Our Lady Immaculate Catholic Church at Tolworth. I had not expected to be 'outed' in this way, but I admitted I was the mystery man at the Mass! The brethren were stunned. We would not have been surprised had Rev. Ron reported converting a Catholic priest, since he was on a roll as far as making converts was concerned, but that one of our number was attending Catholic Mass was beyond belief. After the fuss died down, and Rev. Herbert was asked by the Chairman to stop calling the Mass blasphemous, it was proposed by someone that I should accept the invitation, since it appeared that I was used to fraternising with Catholics. That is how it happened that I went to discuss *Humanae Vitae* with a representative of the Vatican, in the presence of the Apostolic Delegate at his house in Wimbledon. In accepting the invitation I asked if I might bring my wife.

As the day drew near I felt increasing panic. I regard myself as a reasonably competent Baptist minister, proud of having been trained at the oldest Baptist College in the world, but conscious that I failed my

Hebrew examination at Bristol University, and knowing myself to be unable to participate in theological debate at the highest level. I read the English translation of *Humanae Vitae*, on the regulation of birth, but found the argument based on natural law unconvincing. I telephoned the Rev. Dr Leonard Champion, the Principal of Bristol Baptist College, requesting his help. He agreed to meet me at the College.

Dr Champion welcomed me warmly. He said that it would take more than an afternoon for me to master the theological and philosophical subtleties of the Catholic concept of natural law. "Tell them your pastoral experience", was his advice. "You are married, presumably they are not. You have greater understanding of young people's problems than priests in the Vatican. Just share your story with them."

I decided I would wear my black suit and clerical collar for my visit to the Apostolic Delegate. But how does one address a Cardinal? I had seen Catholics kiss a bishop's ring: I was not going to do that! I decided I would approach him with my right hand extended giving him the clue that I anticipated shaking hands. I decided on direct speech, I could not be expected to know how you greet officials from the Vatican. I was a little thrown when the door was opened by a young priest who addressed me as 'Father'. Perhaps it had been a mistake to wear clerical dress. The priest took my coat and Mary's hat, which she had worn because she thought a hat was appropriate for meeting an official from the Vatican!

The Italian Cardinal, I think it was Domenico Enrici who I met, was most courteous. He explained that the

Holy Father had intended that *Humanae Vitae* should be addressed to all people of good will, not only Catholics, and he was wanting to know how English Protestants responded to his encyclical. He thanked me for accepting his invitation and looked forward to hearing what I had to say. I began by expressing my appreciation of the invitation to make a presentation. I assumed that in sending the invitation to a local Baptist Fraternal that he was wanting to have a response from Baptists at a parish level. The Rev. Dr Ernest Payne, General Secretary of the Baptist Union and former Principal of Regents Park College, Oxford, would be the person to give an official response. I asked for the invitation to be extended to my wife since I think it relevant that I am speaking as a married man. We have three children.

I arranged my presentation in three sections. Section One: Pastoral experience in a housing estate at Southend-on-Sea. Section Two: Pastoral experience with marginalised young people in Kingston-upon-Thames. Section Three: Comment on the Encyclical.

SECTION ONE. My first pastorate was in a small Baptist Church in Southend-on-Sea from 1955 to 1961. The membership was around 40 adults. There were half a dozen young adults who had been recently baptised by immersion on profession of faith. They were enthusiastic young Christians. Baptists have a somewhat different lifestyle to Catholics. In theology, Baptists owe more to John Calvin than to Martin Luther. Calvin took from St Augustine the doctrine of predestination. On this basis, Calvin saw humanity to be divided in advance into the Damned and the Elect. He taught that the Christian family could be identified as belonging to the Elect by their rejection of worldly pleasure, their strict sexual morality and abstention from dancing, drinking, gambling and swearing. They are to be hard working, thrifty and therefore prosperous compared to their neighbours. Traces of this theology and lifestyle can be found among Baptists today. In the USA, Baptists aspire to a certain kind of self sufficiency, even prosperity. In the UK, Baptists aspire to be respectable. The ideal Baptist family is husband and wife, two children perhaps, with a nice house and tidy garden. Contraception is taken for granted among Baptists.

In my pastorate at Southend-on-Sea in the 1950's, the young people I ministered to were mainly practising Christians. When an engaged couple came to me to arrange to be married, my wife and I would invite them to have a meal with us at the Manse so that we could share with them our experience of married life. We talked about practical matters like managing money, giving each other space, respecting our differences and sharing responsibilities. At that time we had two children, and naturally spoke of the joys and difficulties of family life. In those days most of the engaged couples on the estate did not live together before marriage, and I believe most were virgins.

We suggested that they might need to have some time to adjust to each other, and grow their own relationship before they embarked on having children. So we encouraged them to visit their local Family Planning Clinic to explore family planning practicalities.

This was not possible in the 1950's unless the minister certified that the date of the marriage had been agreed.

Marriage preparation in my pastoral practice has always been on this informal basis. In most cases these conversations are spaced over a period of about six weeks. As there is no fixed order of service for marriage in Baptist churches, I decide with the couple the words and form of the ceremony.

SECTION TWO. My ministry at the John Bunyan Baptist Church in Kingston-upon-Thames commenced in 1967. The 700-seat Victorian chapel had been regularly full in former times. Although church attendance declined after the war, Baptist churches in suburban areas like Kingston-upon-Thames have often experienced growth. The John Bunyan Baptist Church, however, is situated in the downtown area which has seen massive development of large departmental stores. This church is now isolated, stranded on a traffic island. The question facing the church members when I became minister was: should the remaining church members relocate, uniting with another congregation in the town? Before deciding that question, we needed to ask ourselves if there was a social purpose for us staying on the present site? This attempt to discover our mission lead us to develop a service to hundreds of young people who come into the town centre, especially on Friday nights.

In my presentation to the Apostolic Delegate and other priests, I tried in a few minutes to describe some of the features of the youth rebellion then taking place in South West London. I described the drug scene and the sexual revolution among those young people experimenting with alternative life styles. I explained how the all night Kaleidoscope club, the medical clinic and the prototype hostel, were an attempt to meet the needs of many homeless and alienated people living on the margins of society.

One night, soon after we opened Kaleidoscope, a girl fainted in the club. When I called a doctor who had a connection with our church, he diagnosed her as being pregnant, with serious drug problems and suffering from chronic bronchitis and malnutrition. Finding that the girl was homeless, he doubted if existing health and social services would be able to meet her complex health and social needs. People like her are often found dead while still not yet thirty.

To meet the needs of many of the people attending the Friday night club, Kaleidoscope obtained funding for a clinic run by a doctor and a nurse using a room adjoining the club. In order to prevent unwanted pregnancies, it was decided to offer condoms to individuals identified as vulnerable and at risk. In my presentation, I made it clear that Baptists disapprove of sexual intercourse outside of marriage. The decision of Kaleidoscope to provide condoms to drug addicts and other vulnerable people, was having regard to the multiple problems of their situation, the fact that a child of drug addicts would be difficult to place for adoption, and that for these reasons there would be pressure to terminate any pregnancy.

SECTION THREE. Baptists respond positively to paragraphs in the encyclical which set out the Doctrinal

Principles: God's Loving Design, Married Love, Responsible Parenthood, Union and Procreation. They would not recognise that an act of mutual love which impairs the capacity to transmit life offends against God's design. We share the concern expressed in paragraph 17, that the availability of contraceptives has made marital infidelity easier and contributed to a lowering of moral standards. We do not believe we should urge governments to prohibit the sale of condoms because there is no evidence the public would support such legislation. Baptists believe in the separation of State and Church. Most Baptists believe that the use of contraceptives is a matter to be decided by individual conscience.

Baptists would expect more appeal to Scripture in the encyclical. In referring to the account of God's creation of man in Genesis 1; 26-31, something needs to be said about man being created 'in the image of God.' This implies that humans are meant to be co-workers with God in creation and development. People are meant to have a more comprehensive purpose than simply reproducing and filling up the under populated areas of the earth. God's commandment that men and women are to be 'fruitful and multiply' is linked to the task of 'subduing' the earth and 'having dominion over every living thing'. This means more than animal husbandry being man's responsibility: scientific endeavour, manufacture and distribution, politics and philosophy, and much more besides, are latent within God's creative purpose for humankind. In exercising responsibility for development, the need is for sustainable populations, not unlimited fecundity.

Genesis 2:15-24 gives a fuller description of the purpose of human life. People are not designed solely to cultivate the Garden of Eden. Human beings have rational, moral and spiritual capacities which the story of God's command to Adam not to eat of the tree of knowledge of good and evil illustrates. It is not good to keep people in a state of blissful ignorance, sooner or later they must be given knowledge and freedom to choose. And for this task of rational, moral and spiritual discernment, man needs the companionship of woman.

Mark 10: 1–12 and Matthew 19: 1-12, tell the story of the confrontation between Jesus and the Pharisees on the subject of marriage and divorce, and refers to the creation of man and woman recorded in Genesis. This is the basis for belief in the unitive function of sex: the husband and wife become one flesh. Jesus did not combine the reproductive and unitive functions of sex, and there is no justification in the text for the assertion that both functions must be equally signifi-cant in every act of sexual intercourse.

The Pastoral Directives in the encyclical are addressed to different categories of people: Public Authorities, Christian Couples, and Priests.

Public Authorities are described as 'rulers of nations'. In a democracy, politicians represent those who elect them. Members of Parliament cannot bind themselves to obey the 'natural law' as it is from time to time interpreted by the Magisterium of the Catholic Church. The Church of England, for example, does not pro-hibit the use of contraceptives. If the Catholic Church commands obedience to the teaching authority of the

Church, why should not Muslims demand enforcement of Sharia law in Britain? It is right for the Pope to appeal to public authorities and give moral leadership, but citizens in a democracy will not accept control of the State by the Church.

The appeal to Christian Couples speaks of the inviolable conditions laid down by God's law, and encourages married couples to see 'the fullness of the lay vocation' being to communicate the blessedness of obeying this law. Earlier in the encyclical it states: 'with regard to physical, economic, psychological and social conditions, responsible parenthood is exercised by those who prudently and generously decide to have more children, and by those who, for serious reasons and with due respect to moral precepts decide not to have additional children.' Does this mean, unless there are compelling reasons otherwise, a married couple should go on having more children? Is this the fullness of the lay vocation?

Women who have fifteen years of education may want to run a business, work in a shop, become a politician, be a health professional, a teacher, or a lawyer. Is it virtuous for a married woman to include these ambitions within her understanding of the fullness of her vocation? Is it being a good Christian family for a couple to plan to have only one child, or two, or perhaps a maximum of three?

Catholic priests must teach the moral and dogmatic theology set down by the Magisterium. It is the task of moral and dogmatic theologians to continue the process of making coherent statements of the Christian faith in the light of new knowledge and new situations, but in order that unity may prevail, the Magisterium under the Pope from time to time should set down what is the inspired and authoritative teaching of the Church. The Vatican II Council made clear the collegiate nature of this process and put a new emphasis on the priesthood of all believers. Making a separate appeal to priests and moral theologians must not be seen as implying that lay women and men do not have a special contribution to make in describing God's purposes for married people.

I cannot now remember the discussion which followed my presentation. The purpose of the meeting was not to start a dialogue between Baptists and Catholics; it was simply to gain an understanding of how ordinary Baptists might respond to *Humanae Vitae*. The priests who were present on this occasion were sympathetic to the moral dilemmas we faced in our outreach work at Kaleidoscope. Mary and I left with very positive feelings of having had a warm reception, even if some of our views were at variance with Catholic teaching.

I continued attending the 8 a.m. Mass at Our Lady Immaculate Church when we lived at Surbiton, and later at St Agatha's Church when our family moved into the Kaleidoscope hostel in 1977. My attending Mass was a matter of personal religious devotion; I had not the slightest intention of becoming a Catholic at that time. When Father Derek Vidler was a priest at Our Lady Immaculate Church, we arranged a very successful retreat for about a dozen Catholics and a dozen Baptists from my church. When my church made a public appeal for donations towards the redevelopment of our church site to provide a new chapel, hostel and facilities for Kaleidoscope, we received a generous donation from the Catholic Church at Tolworth which was evidence of a growing relationship between our two churches, while at the same time recognising the delicacy of donating Catholic funds to a Baptist enterprise: the cheque was sent with the dedication, "For the demolition of the existing Baptist Church!"

Another gift signified my affectionate relationship with Father John Cremin, the Parish Priest at St Agatha's. Upon his retirement, Father Cremin sent a cheque with the instruction, "For your work with Irish and other difficult cases!" Undoubtedly, the warmth shown by the Apostolic Delegate, and the good friendships I enjoyed with Father Derek Vidler and Father John Cremin are among the influences which later moved me towards Catholicism.

My meeting with the Apostolic Delegate was some ten years before AIDS became a major concern in developing public health policies. In 1986, Kaleidoscope began supplying syringes to intravenous drug users to discourage the practice of sharing syringes which was likely to spread HIV and hepatitis infections. Our guidelines for this initiative were published by The Standing Conference On Drug Abuse and became accepted as good practice in the UK, and other parts of the world outside of the USA. Anonymous saliva tests showed that this intervention alone had not sufficiently reduced the rate of infection, and our medical staff identified unprotected sex as the main cause of infection. This prompted us to make condoms accessible to everyone in our clinic, not only to those identified as particularly at risk. Anonymous saliva tests have shown that supplying syringes and condoms in combination have successfully reduced HIV among our clients to a level not much different than among the general public.

FORTY YEARS LATER, the meeting with the Apostolic Delegate having taken place around 1970, I am again asked to give my response to *Humanae Vitae*. This time it is my younger son, Martin, who is challenging me to defend my conversion to Catholicism, "How can you accept *Humanae Vitae*? You provided condoms to drug addicts when you were at Kaleidoscope, have you changed your mind?" We often have these mock fights, my younger son and I, usually on the subject of politics: he is Liberal Democrat, I am Labour.

I dig among my papers in the third drawer on the left of my desk, and find my 15-page copy of *Humanae Vitae*. I leaf through the document and find the paragraph I had marked, paragraph 12: "This particular doctrine, often expounded by the magisterium of the Church, is based on the inseparable connection, established by God, which means man on his own initiative may not break, between the unitive significance and the procreative significance which are both inherent to the marriage act."

This is the central teaching, the basis of the whole encyclical: 'the inseparable connection between the unitive significance and the procreative significance, which are inherent' to sexual intercourse. I accept this teaching at the heart of *Humanae Vitae*, and I believe it is a moral foundation for building a truly human community. I want to return to this matter of a moral foundation at the end of this chapter.

The application of the central teaching in this encyclical is where, I believe, there is need for variation to take account of changes in society. I remain convinced of the morality of providing condoms to drug addicts in an attempt to protect vulnerable people, who are at high risk of contracting AIDS. In addition to exceptional conditions which might obtain for particular individuals, I believe there are more general changes in society which call for further reflection, after nearly half a century of rapid social change, on the application of this moral teaching.

Pope Paul VI clearly had in mind Catholic families when he wrote this encyclical. He talks of married people, of the marriage act, and specifically addressed Christian couples. He is speaking as a pastor, like an Italian parish priest in the mid-twentieth century. He might think of a family in a parish who he might call 'blessed': father, mother, three sons and two daughters. He would be aware that there may have been other pregnancies, miscarriages, a stillbirth, or a child who died before the age of 10: these things would not have been uncommon. He would know of the tragedy of a couple who had no child, and of another couple, who for one reason or another, had only one child. He would think it less than desirable for there to be only two children. Three or four children would not call for adverse comment. More than five children might call for congratulations; after eight children there might be cause for reflection. There is the matter of responsible parenthood, "which today, rightly enough, is much insisted upon." Yes, the Parish Priest would be aware of 'man's innate drives and emotions' which might mean that 'man's reason and will must exert control over them'. The Parish Priest would be aware of physical, economic, psychological and social conditions which might demand constraint on the man's part, and consideration for the sensibilities of his wife. If this family of eight children are well off, there is no need to think about responsible parenthood, but if this is a wretched family, living in a slum, in poor health, even a burden on the parish; in such a case the priest should have a word with the Catholic nurse or doctor, to instruct this family in 'recourse to infertile periods'.

That is how I imagine the situation when Pope Paul VI wrote his encyclical. Now the situation is different. Today, women in the parish are likely to express concern among themselves for a woman with three children under the age of five. Those physical, economic, psychological and social conditions are far more relevant today than in previous generations. Most women today have more to do than stay at home and look after babies. There is simply not enough money for the average, and below average, family in Britain to feed, clothe and adequately provide for more than two or three children. Tax payers are no longer willing for the state to subsidise large families and provide suitable accommodation. We are running out of space, water, food and fuel. The application of moral law must vary according to the circumstances.

In the last few decades there has been a significant change with regard to marriage. In former times, most people left school at sixteen and went out to work while living at home. It was normal to 'go courting' in the late teens, and for a girl to marry at nineteen. Child bearing was not normal beyond forty. So there were approximately twenty years of child bearing with the expectation of a number of children. *Humanae Vitae* speaks of the positive value of self discipline and recourse to infertile periods, and in another place, 'recourse to God'. The Pope appeals to scientists to elucidate more thoroughly a proper regulation of birth by natural means. This is sympathetic to the human condition, but much more is now required.

Most young people are in full-time education and career development up to the middle twenties. Marriage is often not considered before the age of thirty. That represents a long pre-marital period of sexual activity. The preferred number of children being two or three, leaves long periods of abstinence, or reliance upon infertile periods which prove unreliable for many couples. These factors have taken the application of the moral law in *Humanae Vitae* to breaking point. Jesus spoke of the religious leaders of his day imposing unbearable burdens upon people. *Humanae Vitae* feels unbearable to more and more people in the circumstances in which they live. The situation calls for reform. In the meantime, Christian couples manage as best they can, but not all the faithful are convinced that there are no alternative applications of moral law than that set out in the encyclical of Pope Paul VI.

My own pastoral experience makes me firmly convinced of the truth of the doctrine, that there is an inseparable connection between the unitive and pro-creative aspects of sexual intercourse. This is the truth which most people can recognise and accept. There is something profoundly unsatisfactory with sexual intercourse which has no intention or desire for a loving relationship, but is simply meant to give pleasure. Such casual relationships are essentially abusive. A person who consents to the intimate and trustful act which rightly belongs to marriage, but finds out after-wards that the partner is ready to move on, is bound to feel abused. In addition to a sense of betrayal, a woman who is abandoned when she is found with child suffers serious injustice. Many men, if they find they have fathered a child, feel injustice if they are denied an active part in bringing up the child.

Many people who enthusiastically embraced features of the 'alternative society' when they were young, are emphatic that the sexual freedom which some pro-claimed proved to be abusive. The films of those days, such as *The L-Shaped Room* and *Billy Liar* reflected and reinforced the '*Sex 'n Drugs 'n Rock 'n Roll*' which Ian Dury sang about. Donovan describes the 'beat girl', 'with no qualms about just sodding off, leaving home and free to take sex where she wants it, without becoming enslaved to a pram.' The Beatles sang, '*she's leaving home*', a ballad about a girl leaving home in the early hours to meet a man in the motor trade. Such freedom led to so much disillusionment and caused so much harm. Kaleidoscope is still treating some of the victims of that culture.

There is need to teach the moral imperative of a long term, loving commitment as a condition for sexual intercourse. The Church rightly requires that this commitment should be within the covenant of Christian marriage, but for those who, for whatever reason, are not willing to marry, or not yet ready to do so, there needs to be a commitment to a long term relationship. Without this minimal foundation, a sexual relationship is likely to be harmful to the individuals concerned, and potentially damaging to society.

7.

Saints Alive

The poet, John Betjeman, had a teddy bear called Archie, who was a Strict Baptist. Archie liked to go to the Baptist Chapel where two Aneucapnic lamps were either side of the pulpit from which the Pastor preached, sometimes for five hours without stopping. The longer the sermon, the more Archie liked it. (*Archie and the Strict Baptists* by John Betjeman).

Being deeply religious himself, it was natural that in humanising Archie, Betjeman would give him a religion. As an undergraduate at Oxford, Betjeman had been drawn to Anglo Catholic worship at Pusey House and continued in that tradition to the end of his life. Betjeman also had a positive experience of Quaker worship, and delighted in the Victorian architecture and fittings of many Free Church chapels. Upon consideration, Betjeman decided that Archie, being a sedentary person, would like sitting, listening to long sermons, rather than genuflecting, standing, sitting and kneeling as was required in the Anglo Catholic Mass. With his keen eye for architectural detail, Betjeman could easily picture Archie sitting in a pew, looking up to the central pulpit with Victorian Aneucapnic oil lamps.

That is what worship largely consists of in many Baptist chapels: sitting, praying, facing the pulpit and listening to Scripture and a substantial sermon. Hymn singing is important, especially in Welsh chapels.

Betjeman liked to attend Mass at St Endellion's church in Cornwall. A. N. Wilson, in his biography of Betjeman, describes the worship at St Endellion's: "The religion is Anglican Catholicism at its most unaffected. There is incense, the priest wears vestments, and the devotion of the church is focused on the Eucharist."

Betjeman, like many other literary people, found Anglo Catholicism powerfully attractive. What is it that scares them off Roman Catholicism? Betjeman's wife, Penelope, was a fervent convert to Roman Catholicism but gave up hoping her husband would convert. In a letter to Evelyn Waugh she explained what hindered her husband from going all the way to Rome: "He thinks Roman Catholicism is a foreign religion which has no right to set up in this country, let alone try to make converts from what he regards as the true Catholic Church of the country." (*Betjeman* by A. N. Wilson, page 173).

The reasons a person joins one church rather than another are indeed complex. C. H. Dodd has given many of the non-theological factors which lead a person to identify with a particular denomination. In the case of Roman Catholicism, the 'foreigness' of that Church is a major factor. There are serious patriotic reasons for English people to be cautious about Roman Catholicism, given the history books most of us grew up with, and the scepticism which many British people feel towards Continental Europe.

For Baptists, quite apart from theological questions, Roman Catholicism is simply alien. Although I have attended Mass regularly for many years, there are still some features of Catholic devotion which are unhelpful to me. My experience on a pilgrimage to Russia helped me overcome some of my religious inhibitions.

I had agreed to advise the Trust of St Francis and St Seraphim on the development of their organisation. The trust has as its aim the promotion of a holistic spirituality, with particular reference to St Francis and St Seraphim. St Francis is well known in Western Europe, but in Eastern Europe, especially in the Sarov region of Russia (450 km North East of Moscow), St Seraphim has been a powerful spiritual influence. St Seraphim spent the first part of his adult life in the Monastery of Sarov, and then lived as a hermit in the forest by the Sarovka river. After many years living in solitude, he was sought out by people who came to him for guidance and healing.

In 1946, Stalin closed the city of Sarov, and in this holy place he built an installation to produce the atom bomb. During this time of brutal persecution of Christians, priests, monks and nuns lived in hiding, but maintained secret places of worship in private homes and in the forest. Following the declaration of perestroika in 1991, St Seraphim's relics were returned to the region, and millions of Russian people lined their route.

One of the activities of the Trust has been to video tape the testimonies of witnesses to persecution during the Soviet period. These testimonies are an invaluable historical and cultural resource. This was the activity which interested me and led to my becoming a Trustee. When Bishop Rupert Hoare resigned as Chair, I undertook that responsibility. It was proposed that in order that I should gain greater understanding of the work of the Trust in Russia, that I should join a Pilgrimage and go on an extended tour to meet the Trust's partners in Russia.

I welcomed the opportunity of visiting Russia and of experiencing Russian Orthodox Church worship, but had it not been for my operational role with the Trust, it is unlikely that I would have gone on a Pilgrimage. Baptists do not do Pilgrimages! The suspicion that there might be an intention to gain merit with God, offends Protestants.

Having decided to go, I found my way to the Russian Orthodox Cathedral in London, to join a group of pilgrims. We had been told to bring layers of clothing because Russia in August can be uncomfortably hot by day and cold by night, and we were told to bring Expedition Plus Insect Repellent because we would be walking in the forest where St Seraphim spent years in prayer. After a briefing, we went into the Cathedral for a blessing. The blessing seemed a bit over the top: every conceivable peril we might encounter was included in the litany chanted by the priest, as his companion repeatedly begged the Lord to have mercy on us!

We flew to Moscow and travelled all night by train through dense forest to Arzamas, and then 70 km in a 4x4 vehicle to Diveyevo. Diveyovo is a small town with a large central area containing a Cathedral, another large church, two monasteries, houses for priests and some shops selling icons and religious books. We stayed in a typical Russian home, not luxurious, but our host was most welcoming with excellent meals made from produce straight from the garden.

The Cathedral of the Holy Trinity in Diveyevo was tightly packed with worshippers when we arrived for the Liturgy next day. Before entering the Cathedral and at significant moments during the service, worshippers made the Orthodox sign of the Cross which signifies the humanity and divinity of Jesus and belief in the Holy Trinity. The congregation in an Orthodox Church stand throughout the long services, but they do not stand still. People seek out a priest to make confession, they write out requests for prayer and they queue to kiss an icon and light a candle.

Orthodox worship resembles Grand Opera: it is a drama with soloists and chorus. This is an ancient way of communicating to a crowd before the invention of microphones. Like opera, it is best to study the plot before you go to the performance. I felt inhibited at first taking part in unfamiliar rituals, but over the next five days, I began to appreciate the physical participation and appeal to all the senses in Orthodox worship.

During these days, we drove in the 4x4 vehicle into the surrounding forest where St Seraphim lived. On one occasion, we came across four men and a woman carrying icons and walking briskly along a path. We had no room in our truck to offer them a lift, but we stopped to talk to them. Unfortunately, our Russian interpreter had difficulty understanding them as they spoke in Church Slavonic and another dialect. It was clear, however, that they urged us to join them on their way to some important event. We walked a few miles, but were glad to get back into our truck when our driver caught up with us. We were given instructions to continue in the same direction for a few more miles.

As we continued on our way, dozens of people joined us on the road. Further on, we saw streams of people coming across fields and tractors bringing whole families; we were all hurrying to some destination still unknown to us. At last we came to a freshly painted church, but the doors were closed and there was a large crowd outside. We waited for a while longer when three cars arrived delivering an Archbishop and several other priests. Monks and nuns were among the crowd outside the restored church.

A great wave of emotion overwhelmed the people as four coffins were brought to the church. The crowd was silent. The Archbishop began to speak. A priest who was with our party interpreted for us. These four coffins contained the remains of four grandmothers, who had been executed on four consecutive nights by a firing squad of soldiers, as punishment for hiding icons and teaching their grandchildren the Christian faith, when prohibited from doing so during the Stalinist revolution. The bodies of these four martyrs had been dug up from their unmarked grave in the forest only a few days before, the grave being located by a survivor of the persecution who had kept the secret until this church had been re-opened. We were present as the newly restored church was about to be consecrated, the relics of the martyrs being placed beneath the altar.

As the coffins were brought towards the church, several old men and women who had witnessed the execution of the four grandmothers, embraced the coffins. They were weeping and triumphant at the same time. They were celebrating the victory of the martyrs over the terror of their persecutors. Our group of pilgrims was transfixed. It dawned on me that I was witnessing the recognition of four contemporary martyrs. Not women who had lived centuries ago, but people who had died for their faith within the living memory of the witnesses I was standing among. As the crowd surged forward to venerate these martyrs, how could I stand aloof?

That was when I first understood the veneration of saints. These were those who had passed through great tribulation and been washed in the blood of the Lamb. The liturgies recalled in the book of Revelation were now open to me. My Protestant inhibitions left me then; and I was now free to enter into the glories of the worship which was about to begin. I no longer have difficulty venerating saints and kissing icons.

This unplanned incident during a pilgrimage in a remote part of rural Russia has had a profound effect on me, but what value can we put on religious practices such as the veneration of saints?

As far as we know, it is unique to humans to be able to remember the past and anticipate the future. Such remembering and anticipating are formative in making us the people we are. This is not only true of us as individuals, but collectively it is true of societies. The suffering of Russian people over many generations is part of their national consciousness. To forget the past, to move on to mundane things without contemplating what happened in former times, can result in superficiality. When I saw young people in Moscow so enthusiastically embracing the consumerism of the West, I wondered if some of the suffering of the past had been in vain. The older generation had suffered grievously through the thorough going adoption of Marxist ideology; was there a danger now of a thorough going adoption of a market ideology? The force that resisted the atheism of the Communist era was the religion of those Christian grandmothers. Within days of the fall of Communism, thousands of churches re-opened in Russia, and millions of Russians reclaimed the spiritual heritage of St Seraphim and all the other saints of the Russian Orthodox Church.

It is easy to give way to the cynicism prevalent in secular society. Many journalists and commentators were perplexed by the outpouring of emotion at the death of Princess Diana. What sophisticated people had overlooked was the high value the public put upon the humanity Diana had often shown, when she visited the homeless, the drug addicts and the victims of AIDS. In a real sense, the Princess was carrying out the teaching of Jesus when he said, "Just as you did it to one of the least of these, you did it to me." The whole of the passage which is the context of that quotation, St Matthew 25; 31 to 41, is the Gospel which Princess Diana often lived out. Those who dismiss her virtues by recalling her faults, show their own hardness of heart.

Humanity, and the rest of the created order, are in urgent need of the kind of creative and compassionate living which true religion can promote. That may not include the veneration of saints and martyrs, but it must of necessity include profound meditation upon the past and a courageous vision for the future.

8.

Becoming a Catholic

I could not help but notice the poster outside the hut near Kingston Hospital: "The Church of God meets here at 11 a.m. on Sundays."

That is an absurd advertisement, suggesting that the Church of God could be contained within that builders' hut. But I understand the belief of the group who meet in that inauspicious building on Sundays: "Where two or three are gathered together in my name," said Jesus, "I am there among them." Potentially, the Church exists wherever two or more believers meet together to share their faith. I can never forget that it was in the non-denominational Central Hall (formally used by a circus) that I came to know Jesus as Lord and Saviour.

It is thought that Christianity reached Rome about AD 50, at least a decade before either Peter or Paul arrived in the city. It is likely that the church was planted in Rome, not by apostles, but by slaves, traders, soldiers or other lay Christians who went from Jerusalem to Rome as prisoners, or on business, and shared their new found faith among themselves and others they associated with.

Of the different groups travelling to Rome, I imagine Roman soldiers being potential carriers of the Christian faith. I remember from my service in the R.A.F. that within a few days of arriving at a new camp, I would have identified and linked up with other evangelical Christians. We would meet together somewhere on camp to study the Bible, to pray, and to encourage each other to keep the faith and spread the Gospel to others. That is how the first Baptist churches were planted in many parts of Britain. Cromwell's New Model Army was largely recruited and officered from Baptists. Soldiers in Cromwell's army included many Puritans who preferred Bible Study to nights at an ale-house, and sought to convert their fellows to Christ, rather than seek out local brothels. Colonel John Rede on his journey to South Wales to stamp out a rising in Pembroke, founded many Baptist churches in the villages on route where his troops were billeted. One of those churches was Porton Baptist Church, near Salisbury, founded in 1640, where I was Student Pastor during the final year of my theological training.

Jesus in his parables of the kingdom of heaven (Matthew 13) chose illustrations from agriculture to describe the growth of God's kingdom. A sower went out to sow, he scattered the good seed here, there and everywhere, and it produced grain in an almost haphazard harvest. Again, referring to someone sowing good seed in a field, the crop is not guaranteed, the wheat is vulnerable and takes its chance along with the weeds, to be sorted at the time of harvest. Again, mustard seed is very small, can easily be spread accidentally, but it grows in its own time and manner, eventually becoming a large shrub, providing food and a nesting place for birds. Yeast is mixed into dough, does its work silently and unnoticed, causing the dough to rise and be ready for baking. This is how the Gospel accomplishes its work, in a mysterious way. The process of evangelisation is unpredictable and there are many different agents. Jesus spoke of the kingdom of God being like wind blowing 'where it chooses' (John 3:8).

Michael Walsh in his scholarly book, *Roots of Christianity* (published by Grafton Books, 1986), gives an account of the origins of the Christian Church in a period prior to the end of the first century, when the Church had not yet established a unified structure. The evidence of the New Testament is that there were different factions. Paul in 1 Corinthians 1:10-17 appeals to the members of the Church at Corinth to be united. He had received reports of quarrels: "I belong to Paul", "I belong to Apollo", "I belong to Cephas", "I belong to Christ". At the high point of his exhortation Paul declares: "All that really matters, in life or death, or the life to come, is that you belong to Christ, and Christ belongs to God" (1 Corinthians 3:23).

The quarrelling in the church at Corinth may have been simply members showing loyalty to one leader, or another. The situation described in Acts, chapters 10, 11, and 15, raised serious theological questions of circumcision, adherence to Jewish laws, and relationships between the apostles at Jerusalem and Hellenists (Greek speaking Christians) at Antioch. These matters were eventually settled when Paul and Barnabas went to Jerusalem to meet with the leaders of the church there. The initiative for the meeting appears to have been Paul's, and the decision process has been called the Council of Jerusalem.

That Peter was leader among the apostles at Jerusalem, there seems no doubt. But Peter did not found the Church at Rome, and there were Christians at Corinth, Ephesus, Antioch and Rome before Paul got there.

The first churches were probably planted by men and women travelling on business from Galilee, Jerusalem and Antioch. Among those who took the Gospel to all parts of the known world, there may have been some of the eyewitnesses who had been in a crowd, or a synagogue, where they heard Jesus preach.

The book of Acts records the rapid expansion of the Church in Jerusalem following the resurrection of Jesus and the gift of the Holy Spirit at the feast of Pentecost. In response to Peter's preaching, almost three thousand people were baptised in a single day. Such mass conversions have been recorded many times in the history of the Church. Almost within living memory is the evangelical revival in Wales in 1904, when thousands were converted listening to the preaching of Evan Roberts, a twenty-six-year-old coal miner. In all such spiritual awakenings, women have had a significant role, which was regarded as threatening the status quo in former times. These spiritual revivals typically produced charismatic, itinerant preachers who spread the message to new communities wherever they went. This is how I imagine the spread of Christianity in the first decades of the early Church.

Michael Walsh notes that, "Paul numbered women among his 'co-workers', and they worked with him on an equal basis. A disagreement between the two women Evodia and Syntyche, recorded in the letter to the Philippians, caused him particular pain because of the major role they had played in spreading the gospel (Phil. 4:2-3). At Rome a large number of women are important enough to be mentioned by name in the last chapter of Paul's letter to the community there."

Catholics tell how Jesus appointed Peter to be the first pope, who handed on the sacred office in an unbroken 'apostolic succession'; that the pope appointed celibate men to be bishops and priests to channel the grace of God to the laity; that a headquarters was established at Rome, and that missions were sent out from there to all parts of the world, establishing churches reporting directly to the hierarchy in Rome.

This narrative is misleading, because it attributes all the initiatives to popes, bishops and priests, and omits reference to the lay men and women who were mainly responsible for spreading the gospel and planting the first Christian congregations. This lopsided version of church history has led at times to clericalism in the Church with bad consequences.

Clericalism is a condition where priests have an exaggerated sense of their importance and sanctity. In extreme cases, they develop 'antinomian tendencies' expressed in a belief that they need not be subject to conventional rules of morality. In the history of the Church there have been good times and bad, but repentance and reform have usually averted schism and widespread immorality among the clergy. By the 16th century. however, immorality among bishops and priests had become common knowledge. All sorts of clerical abuse culminated in selling indulgences which guaranteed relief from punishment in Purgatory.

The Augustinian monk, Martin Luther, was a zealous reformer whose protests lead to unintended consequences. The result was the break up of Christendom into Catholic and Protestant, between those remaining loyal to Rome, and those embracing a variety of forms of Protestantism. A popular opinion among Catholics is that King Henry VIII, a serial adulterer, broke with Rome for a number of ignoble reasons, lust and greed mainly, and that he founded the Church of England. That is another misleading version of events.

What is wrong with these versions of Church history is that they can lead to a sense of spiritual and moral superiority, making repentance and reform less likely. Overlooking the vital role of laymen and women disables the Church in its mission of evangelisation.

Recent celebrations of the 400th anniversary of the Authorised Version of the Bible, reminded me of my training at the Bristol Baptist College, and the association with William Tyndale, whose translation of the New Testament and parts of the Old Testament, accounts for the greater part of the text of the Authorised Version. I remember racing downstairs at college to the sound of Big George, the university bell, calling us to lectures on the ground floor of the college, or across the road to the university. As I leapt, two stairs at a time, I could not avoid seeing the huge stained glass window which occupied almost the entire right hand wall of the staircase, depicting the life and martyrdom of William Tyndale. It is surely ironic that Tyndale, the Puritan reformer, is commemorated in a stained glass window! More evocative was the knowledge that a first edition of his translation of the New Testament was kept in the college safe (since sold to the British Museum). I am still on the side of William Tyndale and against Cardinal Wolsey who burnt copies of Tyndale's translation with religious ritual and consented to that ghastly martyrdom at the stake. Tyndale was right in believing that a plough boy if he read the New Testament in his own language would see that indulgences, relics and Purgatory were missing from the New Testament, and that the excesses of priests were in stark contrast to the simple life of Jesus and his disciples.

My first reading of the New Testament gave me a simple picture of Jesus and his disciples. It was not until my theological training that I was aware of references in the New Testament to bishops and deacons. It was not until I read translations of documents of the early Church that I learned of the earliest Eucharistic liturgies. It was not until I read of Ignatius and Polycarp that I began to understand the role of bishops in the early Church. At college, I began to understand how the Church developed beyond the period of itinerant preachers. I read some of St. Augustine and Thomas Aquinas, but as you would expect from a Baptist college, I learned more of Luther, Calvin and Zwingli. During my final year, I studied the works of Karl Barth and Emil Brunner, two of the greatest Protestant theologians of the twentieth century. In my last term I discovered Dietrich Bonhoeffer. After five years of training at a Baptist theological college, I was a Conservative Evangelical without any inclination towards Catholicism.

I believe the word of God, the Gospel of Jesus Christ, has been spread widely and unsystematically, being blown about by the Holy Spirit in many surprising ways. I do not believe that only those plantings and fruitings which occurred under the supervision of a bishop are wholesome grain. Nevertheless, I believe that the visible unity of the Church is God's will, and that the Catholic Church with its hierarchical structure under the Pope, has the potential to bring salvation to the world.

I liken my decision to join the Catholic Church to Paul's decision to go up to Jerusalem to receive the 'right hand of fellowship' from Peter and the other leaders of the Church. Paul describes this decisive moment in his life in the second chapter of Galatians. His decision was in response, Paul tells us, to a revelation. Paul does not describe how God's will that he should go to Jerusalem was disclosed to him; whether directly to him, or through some other person. It seems unlikely that he would have woken up one morning and said to Barnabas and Titus, his fellow missioners, "God has told me we must go up to Jerusalem." It seems more probable, that having discussed with his companions the accusation against them that they were not authorised by the Apostles, that Paul declared his conviction that they should go to Jerusalem to have this matter settled once and for all. Paul was convinced that God required him to seek unity with Peter and the other apostles. Reading the account in Galatians, I detect a struggle going on in his mind. Paul had considerable misgivings about referring this matter for decision "at the highest level". We can almost see his 'body language' when he says in an aside, "those who were supposed to be acknowledged leaders (what they actually were makes no difference to me)!" Paul goes into the meeting, protesting: "what I have done over fourteen years of ministry, walking thousands of miles over rough roads, putting up with a great deal of hardship and pain, was not all in vain because it was not authorised by Jerusalem!" Paul will not yield an inch to anyone, his Christian experience was authentic, undeniable and God given. Whatever his misgivings, Paul knew what he had to do. He recognised in that decisive moment, that moment of revelation, that church unity was an imperative of the Gospel.

My decision was not as dramatic as that. There was no decisive moment, no revelatory experience, only a nagging going on in my head since ecumenical encounters in the 1950's and 60's. Baptist colleagues of mine, members of the Baptist Renewal Group, will remember how we used to talk about entering into a covenant with Christians of other denominations. I never lost that vision. During the final few years of my twenty-seven years of ministry in Kingston-upon-Thames, I saw the disintegration of the Church in many places. Protestantism, the Free churches and more recently the Church of England, seemed to me to be falling apart. William Naphy in his book, *The Protestant Revolution* (published by BBC books 2007) speaks positively of the legacy of the Reformation, but concludes: "Protestantism replaced a mechanism of authority with a recipe for chaos" (page 263). That was my perception. What distressed me, was the utter chaos of disunity and the consequent failure of the churches to speak the Word of God to the world. We sang: 'One Faith, One Lord, One Church', but we continued to assert our own autonomy.

I did not come to the decision to become a Catholic without a struggle. I could not have become a Catholic if it meant repudiating the reality of my Christian faith as a Baptist. It was never my intention in attending Mass while I was still a Baptist Minister, that one day I would become a Catholic. My call to become a disciple of Jesus as a teenager in Northampton was real. My call to become a Baptist Minister and my ordination were real and valid. My half century of ministry had not been in vain. I did not come to my decision on my own. My wife, Mary, shared my dilemma, but the person to help us move on was a nun.

Sr. Frances Makower was brought up as a Liberal Jew and educated at Roedean School and Oxford, where she read history. She became a Roman Catholic in 1952 and joined the Society of the Sacred Heart in 1967. After teaching for many years, Frances was forced to give up due to growing disability from a back injury. After a period of therapy, she came to work at Kaleidoscope. She wrote about her experience in *Faith or Folly* (DLT 1989).

What Frances could not do because of severe physical disability, she more than made up for by her formidable determination. When Frances came to work at Kaleidoscope, she insisted on doing all the tasks required of staff, including domestic chores. She also sought permission from her spiritual director and her community to attend our worship. I remember the occasion when I asked her to put in her words what transubstantiation meant to her. She records her answer, "Christ is present in so many different and unexpected ways, but when I receive the Lord in Holy Communion he is tangibly (officially, if you like) present; through grace, he actually becomes an inseparable part of my being and yet paradoxically it is at that moment that I am enabled to reach out beyond myself to become a part of the whole Body of Christ, of all humankind" (page 18-19).

On another occasion, Frances records hearing me preach on the Real Presence: "He used the analogy of a disused lighthouse that had been turned into a home. Its original use had been transformed, so it was no longer a lighthouse, yet its outer structure had not changed and to the uninitiated it remained a lighthouse" (page 19). Frances says that she was astonished at my sacramental theology. This description of theological dialogue was typical of the many opportunities we had of sharing together the meaning of Christian belief and discipleship. By entering fully into the life of Kaleidoscope and of the John Bunyan Baptist Church, without in the least compromising her dedication as a Roman Catholic religious sister, she opened up the way for Mary and me to explore Catholicism.

It became clear from our conversations that Frances and I were in substantial agreement about the meaning of the Eucharist. The main, and important, difference was that Frances was at all times conscious of her obligation to think and act 'in harmony' with her Order and with Rome; I was accountable to the members of a local church, with only an undefined relationship with the 'invisible' Church of God. By analogy, the contrast is like that between independent traders, and members of a corporate body. I came to see the importance of being a member of a properly constituted body under universal command; rather than being an individual believer with only a loose attachment to an 'invisible' church. I was beginning to accept the importance of episcopacy.

Perhaps it helped, that Frances by temperament did not find obedience to her Order easy. Her Jewishness was apparent, and her self-will was often difficult for her to control. I am a Cockney (the word is said to refer to something slightly misshapen!), I too find it difficult to obey or even to belong. The Latin Church is not my natural habitat. But Frances had learned that Christian discipleship means "making every effort to maintain the unity of the Spirit in the bond of peace" (Ephesians 4:3). That unity and that bond was part of Christian discipleship I had not yet learned.

The Apostle Paul saw that it would be a grave error for him to continue as an independent evangelist, perhaps becoming the founder of a Pauline faction. He rightly concluded that Peter and the other apostles were the centre of unity for the Church. As a disciple of Jesus it was incumbent upon Paul to receive 'the right hand of fellowship' from Peter. Putting aside any reservations, that is what he did. And that is what I decided to do. My first action was to telephone Frances to ask her the telephone number of her spiritual director, Fr Patrick Purnell SJ, so that I could ask him for instruction for Mary and myself to determine whether or not we could in conscience become Catholics.

When Paul went up to Jerusalem to meet with Peter and the other Apostles, the basic question to be decided was, what is required for a person to be justified before God? According to many of the Jewish believers who had become Christians, circumcision and other Jewish obligations were required, as well as faith in Jesus as Saviour and Lord. At the Council of Jerusalem (Acts 15:1-29), the Apostles listened attentively to Paul and his companions who testified to God's grace bringing Gentiles into a right relationship with God through faith in Jesus Christ. It was evident that God had made no distinction between Jewish and Gentile Christians, both were saved through the grace of God manifested in Jesus Christ.

When Mary and I went to meet Fr Patrick Purnell SJ, the obvious matter to discuss was the doctrine of Justification by Faith, which is generally believed to have been the theological issue which caused the split between Protestants and Catholics in the first place. Although this might have been the foremost issue, in fact it was not. This issue had been thoroughly examined by the eminent Catholic theologian, Hans Kung, in his book, *Justification*. In that book, which I read when it was published in English (Thomas Nelson & Sons, 1964), Kung examined the doctrine of grace as Karl Barth, the foremost Protestant theologian, had defined in his ten volumes of Church Dogmatics. Kung showed that between Barth and Catholicism there is fundamental agreement on this issue. I cannot claim parity of reasoning with Barth or Kung, but my reading of Kung's book satisfied me that when it comes to our justification before God, neither Catholic nor Baptist dare stand on any other ground than the abundant grace of God.

Episcopacy was the crucial issue for me in deciding to be a Catholic. The Reformers of the 15th and 16th centuries had not intended to destroy the unity of the Church. Radical groups, such as Baptists, had given liberty to fellowships to interpret scripture under the guidance of the Holy Spirit, not as anyone saw fit. Authority was given for local churches to administer Baptism and the Lord's Supper according to the patterns given in the New Testament. There had never been the intention that believers should have choice in joining and leaving fellowships as they pleased. It was to guard against a drift towards a loose fellowship of independent congregations that the Baptist Union was founded in 1913.

The Rev. John Shakespeare, the first General Secretary of the Baptist Union, set about creating out of independent congregations, something more like a Church body. He went on to advocate a united Church, and in his final address to the Baptist Union he declared, "It is no use concealing my conviction that re-union will never come to pass except upon the basis of episcopacy". It was not until 1951, when Dr Ernest Payne became General Secretary that Baptists again had strong leadership towards Church unity. In 1964, the British Council of Churches proposed that the member churches covenant or unite by 1980. But soon after, the Baptist Union rejected the proposal. Again, it was episcopacy which was the major obstacle.

Episcopacy is a dirty word among Baptists. Bishops in time past exercised power over the bodies, minds and souls of people. They contradicted the concept of Christian Liberty which John Milton passionately espoused and Baptists practiced. Many Baptist churches were founded by lay people; mill owners, shopkeepers and independent traders. These lay people did not want to cede power to ecclesiastical authorities, neither did their ministers want to come under the authority of bishops.

This matter of episcopacy should be decided on the authority of the New Testament, not rejected out of hand because of a misuse of power in former times, because property owners are unwilling to give up control, or because Free Church ministers are unwilling to give up their autonomy. It is clear from the New Testament that Jesus appointed twelve Apostles to lead the Church, among whom Peter, James and John were an inner group chosen by Jesus as a kind of hierarchy. The meaning of the verse "You are Peter and on this rock I will build my Church" (Matthew 16:18), can still be debated, but in the Acts, and in the Pauline Epistles, it is clear that Peter was the leader of the Church. The unity of the Church which Christ prayed for, and which is the gift of the Holy Spirit, gave rise to Paul's description of the Church, as the body of Christ. Like any human body there are disfigurements, but the creeds and liturgies of the early Church are an authoritative source for what Christians believe today, and provide, in outline at least, for a common liturgy.

Vatican II Council (1961 to 65), was a demonstration of episcopacy within the Roman Catholic Church shown on television and reported in newspapers at the time. There were creative debates, with proper tensions evident in deliberations between cardinals and bishops. Priests and lay people joined in the debates at local locations. Although the concept of collegiality needs to be further developed and implemented, there is a recognition that teaching is a two way process of communication. There is a requirement for parish priests to defer to bishops, and for bishops to act according to the conclusions reached by cardinals and pronouncements by the Pope, but the hierarchy must listen to the laity who also are the People of God. This relationship of obedience and trust is such a demanding discipline that a degree of failure is inevitable in any human body. This is why at every Mass prayers are said for the Pope, bishops, clergy and the entire people of God. It is a triumph of grace whenever episcopacy works, and evidence of human failure when it does not.

The great Baptist leader of the 19th century, Rev. John Shakespeare, challenged Baptists to overcome their opposition to episcopacy, but they were not prepared to go that far, Shakespeare lost support, and died a disappointed man. The great Baptist leader of the 20th century, Dr Ernest Payne, in his final address to the Baptist Union declared that the denomination was at a critical moment, and passionately called upon them to go forward with the movement towards church unity.

I had several meetings with Dr Payne, who encouraged me during my campaign for the liberation of Angola and in my ministry at Kingston. I know he was disappointed when Baptists held back from moving forward towards Church unity.

With the help of Fr Patrick Purnell SJ, Mary and I finally decided to petition the Bishop of Menevia for us to be received into the Catholic Church. At a weekday Mass at St Teilo's Church in Tenby on 2nd December 2006 we were received into the Church by Mgr Brian Kinrade. In his homily, Fr Patrick Purnell declared that it would be wrong to call us converts as we had been baptised members of the Church of Jesus Christ for many years, and I had been an ordained Baptist minister for over fifty years. Mary was so moved by the occasion, and by Fr Purnell's homily that she went over to him and kissed him!

I bless God for the gracious and persistent wind of the Holy Spirit that has in time driven me over the great divide between Protestantism and Catholicism, and brought me to unity in the One, Holy, Catholic and Apostolic Church of God. In the last decade or more of our lives together, Mary and I have not been disappointed, but have come home to a beautiful place.

9

Ave Maria

Nothing can prepare a Protestant for the encounter with the Virgin Mary in the Catholic Church. Whereas most doctrines are common to all Christian churches, there are a number of dogmas about Mary that are peculiar to the Catholic Church. Apart from the Hail Mary prayer during the intercessions, there are only sparse references to Mary in the Mass. A Protestant is likely to feel uncomfortable with some of the hymns about Mary, but as time goes by, the convert is arrested by the practice of praying to Mary and venerating her.

At the Vatican II Council there was a move to check a surge in Marian devotions which occurred during the nineteenth century, with the reported apparitions at Lourdes, Fatima and elsewhere. Although the Council focused the Church on the Bible, and in this way discouraged excess of Marian devotion, the Council came out in favour of giving Mary the title of Mother of the Church. There can be no doubt that the Virgin Mary occupies a prominent position in the Catholic Church.

Liberal Protestants during the nineteenth century tended to narrow down their reading of the Gospel to the life of Jesus, from the beginning of his public ministry at his baptism, and ending with his death on the cross. Liberal Protestant ministers are likely to refer to Mary only at Christmas.

Protestants and Catholics define themselves not only by what they believe, but also by what they do not believe. What Protestants definitely do not believe is Catholic dogmas and devotions associated with Mary. That is why becoming a Catholic is a culture shock to someone, like me, who has been a Protestant for most of their life. And it is why, I turn now to the subject of the Virgin Mary.

Protestants object to the ascription of merit to Mary. In this regard the words of Augustine are relevant: 'the teaching of predestination hampers and ruins only one thing: the pernicious error which would have it that the gift of grace depends on our merits'. Any idea that the Virgin Mary, or any other human being, can store up merit which can be traded with God to obtain his favour is a pernicious error. This clarifies an important matter, the truth about Mary hinges upon the belief that she was predestined, chosen, to give herself, even her body, to God in love, in response to God's love for her. It is all a matter of grace. The Hail Mary prayer begins with this acknowledgement of the grace of God: "Hail Mary, full of grace!"

God's choice of Mary is confirmed in the prayer known as The Angelus. This prayer, well known to Catholics, recalls the visit of the angel Gabriel to Mary declaring that she had been chosen by God to conceive, by the Holy Spirit, and bear a son to be named Jesus (Luke 1:26-38). The Church did not elevate Mary; God exalted her.

That God predestined Mary to be the mother of Jesus must not be interpreted in such a way as to deprive her of responsibility, or freedom of choice. Mary had the choice to turn away from God's calling. The reason why every generation shall call Mary blessed is because she said yes to God's will: 'Be it done to me according to your will'. That is why Catholics honour Mary.

Protestants have difficulty with praying through Mary to God. A fundamental principle of Protestantism is that each individual is accountable to God and can have immediate access to him. There is no need of a 'middle man or woman' as it were, Jesus is the only mediator between God and humankind. This truth needs to be enlarged upon, because it was not God's will simply to save individuals in a spiritual manner; God created men and women to be a 'people' for himself. For this reason, God in his Son needed to be incarnated into the human race; he needed to be born of a woman. Human beings are essentially social. A baby begins out of a union between a man and a woman, the baby has multiple relationships with others and cannot develop as a moral person without being in a community. Mary is the first member of God's new community.

Just as a baby becomes a member of a family in the first instance by its relationship with its mother, so Mary helps us realise we belong to God's family. Mary is Mother of the Church, through her we begin to experience the Church as the community into which we have been born by the Holy Spirit. There is a danger in Protestantism that a believer may never develop an adequate sense of being incorporated into the Church. Devotion to Mary has given me a greater consciousness of belonging to God's Church.

Any honour given to Mary is a reflection of the honour given to her by God. God's ultimate purpose is to make himself manifest in the lives of those who are being redeemed. Paul says of all believers that we work together with Christ (2 Corinthians 6:1). A person could hardly be more of a co-worker with Christ in his redemptive purpose than to carry him in their womb until full term! John Macquarrie, referring to Mary's part in the drama of salvation, says, "a part which I have not hesitated to call 'indispensable'." (page 3 *Mary For All Christians*, Collins reprint 1992). This is why I have come to acknowledge Mary without reservation, wholeheartedly, and with true devotion.

IMMACULATE CONCEPTION

> "Chosen from eternal ages,
>   you alone of all our race,
>   by your Son's atoning merits
>   was conceived in perfect grace."

That verse of a hymn neatly expresses the doctrine of the immaculate conception of the Virgin Mary. The doctrine has developed out of the belief that God chose Mary from the beginning, and that God redeemed her from the moment of her conception.

Scripture says we are chosen in Christ "before the foundation of the world to be wholly and blameless before him in love" (Ephesians 1:4). On this basis, we affirm that God blessed Mary with grace, appropriate to her role of being the mother of Jesus, from the beginning. It is God's purpose to bring the whole of creation, including all humanity, to perfection. But we know that humans repeatedly fall from that perfect will of God. This observation about the universality of human failure leads to belief in 'original sin', that the human race has inherited sinfulness from our first parents, Adam and Eve. In pre scientific times this was described as a 'stain', located in the blood perhaps, which is responsible for the human propensity to sin. A degree of reservation about original sin is necessary, otherwise all bad behaviour can be blamed on our forefathers, and not our responsibility. It must remain a possibility that a person could be born whose character was blameless, especially if you factor in a unique calling and endowment of the Holy Spirit.

In considering this theological concept of original sin being a 'stain', John Macquarrie has suggested using instead the modern concept of alienation. If we think of sin as being alienation from God, alienation from other people, even alienation within ourselves, then it is possible to think of Mary being without any such alienation from God and other people. Indeed, the biblical account is that she gave herself unreservedly to God in response to the call of the angel Gabriel, she gave her body that the Christ-Child should be implanted in her womb. She gave herself for the redemption of humanity. Such unique and unreserved response to God makes it credible to speak of her being immaculate. It is this uniqueness of God's grace and Mary's complete self giving which is celebrated in the first part of the Hail Mary prayer:

Hail Mary, full of grace,
the Lord is with thee,
blessed art thou among women
and blessed is the fruit of thy womb, Jesus.

THE ASSUMPTION

I was in the RAF at the time. The year was 1950. I had heard on the News that Pope Pius XII had promulgated the dogma of the Assumption of the Blessed Virgin Mary. That was all I needed. I hurried to breakfast in the Mess, excited by the thought of confronting my Roman Catholic friend: "How can you possibly believe that Mary was assumed 'body and soul' to heaven? The very idea is ridiculous; can a human body float up into outer space? And, this is the important point, where do you find this in the Bible?" My friend had obviously anticipated my challenge. He countered, "I thought you believed that you would go to heaven? Why do you think that the mother of Jesus would not go to heaven?"

We did not pursue the matter further, we knew that both Protestants and Catholics alike have difficulty interpreting what exactly we mean by phrases like 'going to heaven' and 'bodily resurrection'. Both of us were Radar Fitters, who knew that scientific technology could not locate heaven in the sky.

As a Baptist minister I have had to think seriously and deeply about what I mean when at a funeral I pronounce: "Forasmuch as it hath pleased almighty God to call away from this life the soul of our dear one, we therefore commit his/her body to the ground, earth to earth, ashes to ashes, dust to dust, and leave his/her soul with God, his/her maker and Saviour in sure and certain hope of the resurrection to life immortal, through our Lord Jesus Christ, who died and is risen again, and is even at the right hand of God."

What is the basis of my sure and certain hope in the resurrection to life immortal? As a young Christian, I believed in eternal life because of the statement in John's Gospel, chapter 3, verse 16: "For God so loved the world that he gave his only Son, so that everyone who believes in him may not perish but may have eternal life." As the years have passed, I have given more thought, reflecting upon the significance of God 'remembering me'. If I am in the mind of God who loves me, he will surely want me to live with him for ever. This thought is contained in a number of well known verses. Luke 23:42: the dying criminal next to Jesus on the cross, said, "Jesus, remember me when you come into your kingdom." He replied, "Truly I tell you, today you will be with me in Paradise." John 17:24: Jesus prayed, a short time before his death, "Father, I desire that those also, whom you have given me, may be with me where I am, to see my glory, which you have given me because you loved me before the foundation of the world." If I believe that, I believe that of Mary the mother of Jesus, only more so. She bore Jesus in her womb, she held him close to her in life and in death, she was uniquely drawn to him at the end of her earthly life.

In what way is the Assumption of Mary different from the Ascension of Jesus? The Ascension of Jesus is the inescapable consequence of our Lord's divinity. Jesus "came down from heaven: by the power of the Holy Spirit he became incarnate of the Virgin Mary, and was made man." As long as he was human he was subject to death, but at the closure of his earthly ministry, he rightfully resumed his undivided relationship with the Father. It is not the same with Mary. She did not 'come down from heaven', she was not a person in the Godhead. When she died, she died as every other human. But at the moment of her mortal death, she was 'assumed' (taken up) into God, by a signal act of God.

In what way is the Assumption of Mary different from the 'going to heaven' of all believers? In many respects it is not different. St Paul in 1 Corinthians, chapter 15, verses 51 to 53: tells us it is a mystery! Referring to those who are still alive at the return of Christ he says, "we will not all die," but he affirms that we will all be changed; "For the trumpet will sound, and the dead will be raised imperishable, and we will be changed. For this perishable body must put on imperishability, and this mortal body must put on immortality." Again, referring to the end time, the writer of 1 Thessalonians, chapter 4, verse 17, declares: "Then we who are alive, who are left, will be caught up in the clouds together with them to meet the Lord in the air; and so we will be with the Lord for ever." This theological language, using figurative words and human time frames, describes an assumption of the faithful at the return of Christ in glory. These quotations show that there is not an essential difference, but there is a significant difference: Mary is unique in being,

I can think of no other way of putting it, a 'prototype' of every believer. As a prototype, Mary demonstrates our own 'being taken to God' at the end of our lives.

DEVOTIONAL REFLECTION

I have lived most of my Christian life without the mother of Jesus being particularly significant to me. The writers of the gospels of Mark and John hardly mention the Virgin Mary. Revelation 12:1-6 look like a description of the Virgin Mary exalted in heaven, but otherwise there is no evidence of a devotion to Mary in the epistles. Jose Antonio Pagola, in his scholarly book, *Jesus An Historical Approximation* (Convivium 2009), makes only scant reference to Mary. The story of Jesus can be told without saying much about his mother.

When people began reading the Bible for themselves at the Reformation, they found features of Catholicism which were not in the New Testament. An excess of Marian devotion has been a cause of offence to many 'bible loving' Christians.

Evangelical Christians talk of a personal relationship to Jesus. This personal emphasis can lead to prayer becoming a conversation between me and Jesus. That is not a bad thing, but it is egocentric. Prayer is better addressed to, "almighty God and Father", in the consciousness of having access to God through Jesus Christ "Son of the Father", who alone is Holy and takes away the sin of the world; and in the knowledge that the Holy Spirit speaks for us to the Father.

Where, therefore, in this awesome Trinity, is there a place for Mary?

The book of Revelation contains a first Prayer Book of the Christian Church, and Chapter 4 provides the setting with the focus upon the throne. "The throne," to quote my former tutor, Professor Kenneth Grayston, "means not simply the ceremonial seat of majesty but Majesty itself. The twenty-four elders act as a kind of Privy Council whose chief duty is to articulate praise (and therefore approval) of the divine acts of creation and redemption" (*Dying we Live*, Kenneth Grayston, DLT 1990). We must not think of prayer as a private audience with God; a whole 'cloud of witnesses' are present with us. Mary, the mother of Jesus, the apostles, the martyrs, the saints, all those who have gone before us in the faith are with us. When I am up against ecclesiastical authority, I look to St Joan of Arc. When I am beaten up emotionally, I look to St Seraphim. When I can't fix the electrics, I look to my father who was an electrician and died a believer in Christ. When I have a problem with wood, I look to my father-in-law who was a carpenter and knew God before he died.

The dogmas of the Immaculate Conception, and the Glorious Assumption give an exalted place for the Virgin Mary in the prayer life of the Church. Mary does not impinge upon the redeeming work of Christ. We look to Jesus for our salvation, but we may look to Mary as one who learned to exercise perfect faith in God. Luke tells the story of the twelve-year-old Jesus being lost in the Temple and found talking to the teachers (Luke 2: 41 to 51). On this and other occasions Mary and Joseph did not understand Jesus. We can identify with Mary in her coming to terms with God's role for Jesus in redeeming humanity. Never more so, than in her witnessing the cruel death of her son in his dying agony. This is why Mary takes a prominent place in the prayer life of Catholics. We learn to love God through contemplating the sufferings of Jesus, and we learn to contemplate the sufferings of Jesus by imagining what Mary went through. That is the heart of the devotion known as Stations of the Cross, and Mary's standing at the foot of the cross is the theme of many hymns.

Not only does Mary bring us closer to Jesus; Mary brings Jesus closer to us. In our weakness, in times of trouble, in facing peril and in our hour of death, we gather strength from the weakness, the distress and the despair that Mary, the mother of Jesus, knew.

Revelation, chapter 12:1-6, with the vision of a woman clothed with the sun, with the moon under her feet, and on her head a crown of twelve stars, would appear to be a description of the Virgin Mary exalted to heavenly splendour. Who else gave birth to the Son who is destined to be Lord of Lords and King of Kings? The Archangel Michael and a host of other angels are mentioned in verse 7. This vision looks back to the birth of Jesus, sees the present conflict between the powers of good and evil, and sees into the future predicting the ultimate triumph of God. This mystical, Jewish-Christian-Persian imagery is not to everyone's taste, and certainly literal minded Protestants would look askance at it, but this is the kind of other world poetry which is included in the prayer life of the

Catholic Church. Minimalist Protestants can do without these visionary extravagancies; but I doubt if religious faith can flourish in worship expressed exclusively in down to earth prose.

Having been released from the constraints of liberal Protestantism, I am discovering a much richer prayer life as a Catholic. I still like to exercise my own judgement in many matters of faith, but I want now to live in communion with the Church of Jesus and his apostles and their successors, with Mary, the mother of Jesus, and with all the Saints, obedient to the call to Catholic unity of the People of God.

I believe Catholicism has the potential to be a model of the unity which should be the goal of all nations. I believe the Vatican II Council with its decisions on collegiality and subsidiarity has signposted the way forward. I do not imagine an imminent fulfilment of the vision of the Kingdom of God, but I hope, even in my late stage of life, to be able to participate in the mission of the Church, to bring reconciliation and fulfilment to people on earth.

10.

When Marriages Fail

Our family were sympathetic to Mary and I becoming Roman Catholics. I think they saw it coming, especially since we had not found a Baptist Church in Pembrokeshire where the Eucharist was central to the worship. The two fundamental theological issues between Protestants and Catholics are, 'Justification by Faith' and 'Transubstantiation'. The first of these issues had been resolved for me when I read Hans Kung's great book, *Justification*, soon after its translation into English (Thomas Nelson, 1964). The second, transubstantiation, I had resolved in my own mind long before I expounded that doctrine in my own small book, *Permission to Be*, published by DLT in 1992. Catholics are usually taught that Protestants do not believe in the 'Real Presence', but that in fact is not true of a great many Protestants.

My younger son, Martin, repeatedly challenges us: "Surely you don't believe in the infallibility of the Pope? Martin knows that I could not believe that anything the Pope might say is infallible. In fact, papal infallibility is limited to what the Pope by a definitive act proclaims as doctrine pertaining to faith or morals. The Pope does not act alone. The Pope is Peter's successor, and the bishops are the successors of the apostles, and these are related and united to one another. It is called collegiality. This I do believe.

"You do not accept *Humanae Vitae!*"

He knows I agreed to providing condoms to drug addicts at our Kaleidoscope clinic.

"You do not accept Catholic teaching on Marriage and Divorce, surely?"

Well, I am trying to get my head round the bewildering Canon Law on these matters.

Martin at his own request at the age of twelve, had asked to be transferred from a State Comprehensive School to the Richard Challoner Catholic School when we lived in Kingston. He hugely enjoyed the school, and his form teacher, an Irish woman, told Mary and me, "Ah, Martin would make a lovely Catholic!" Martin, now a Baptist Minister, came to the service at St Teilo's Catholic Church when Mary and I were received into the Church, he read one of the lessons, and he has on more than one occasion accompanied us to Mass. He is not antagonistic to the Catholic Church, but I don't think he is ready to join any time soon!

The problem with Catholic teaching on marriage and divorce is well illustrated in the case of a friend of ours. She was married for a number of years, husband and wife both Catholics, married in the Catholic Church. They had three children, but just at an age when their daughter was playing up, her husband abandoned them. In due course, they were divorced and sometime after he met another woman. After what seemed to her a fairly short time, her ex-husband obtained an annulment and married the new woman in a Catholic Church where they both regularly attend and take the sacrament at Mass. She demands an answer to her question, "How can the Church say I was never really married?"

All churches are facing the same increased incidence of divorce among their members. Programmes on television showing how life used to be in Victorian times remind us that working class men used to start work in mines, factories, shops and offices at 8 a.m. at the latest. Arriving home at the earliest at 6 p.m., he read the newspaper, then washed his hands while his wife dished up the evening meal. After his meal, the man often left home again, having eaten and changed, going to the Public House where he played dominoes and darts, or going to band practice in Northern towns, or choir practice in Welsh chapels. A variety of Working Men's Clubs, fraternities, amateur groups, bowls and Union meetings were some of the activities which kept men away from home until the babies were settled and the children gone to bed. If it was a happy marriage, the couple sat together by the fire for an hour before bed time. If it was an unhappy marriage, the man came home late, possibly drunk and abusive. Many couples survived like that till death parted them. The law on marital rape was only recently reformed. Today, it is practical for a woman to obtain a divorce. Men and women can escape a loveless marriage by means of divorce. Many find a more fulfilling life with a new partner.

The churches are unanimous in teaching that marriage is a life long union of one man and one woman. But what is to be done when a marriage breaks down? The Parish Priest, relatives and friends, and marriage guidance counsellors do their best in seeking a reconciliation. Sometimes the couple themselves, mindful of the positives in their relationship, resolve their difficulties. But when all efforts fail, what is to be done when it is apparent that the situation is irretrievable? And what is to be done if the couple separate, are divorced, find new partners and want to be married in church?

The Church faces a dilemma. In the beginning, in Genesis 2:24, it is recorded that a man and a woman united in marriage become one flesh. Jesus not only confirmed this, but he rejected divorce declaring, "What God has joined together let no man separate." (Mark 10:9).

Belief that the marriage bond is lifelong and indissoluble is not unique to Catholics. What is unique to Catholics is their legal system, which finds it possible to declare that many people, who thought they were married and were sexually active over a period of years together, were not really married in the first place! Our friend, who still identifies herself as a Catholic and has nearly come to terms with the fact that her ex-husband now lives with another woman, continues to feel outrage that the Church has declared that her marriage over 13 years was not valid. Our friend is only one of many in her situation, the pain of those who petition for an annulment and are unsuccessful is also acute. They are forbidden to marry again, or if they do, they are denied holy communion for life.

It falls to the members of the Diocesan Tribunal to consider the evidence when a petition for an annulment is lodged. Is there evidence that consent was defective when the man or the woman said, "I will"? Was the bride pregnant at the time, and under pressure to get married? Was the man under pressure to do the decent thing? Had one or other of the couple made a foolish promise sometime before and felt unable to back out when the wedding had been arranged? Did the woman feel there was no other choice? Did the man get married in a hurry because he was being sent overseas by the army? Was one of the partners homosexual and agreed to the marriage in order to be 'normal'? It is not enough to show that consent may have been defective, there must be evidence that consent was seriously defective.

There are other possibilities. Could this case be resolved under what is known as 'The Pauline Privilege'? It is recorded in 1 Corinthians 7: 10 to 16, that St Paul, mindful of Christ's teaching that in marriage a man and a woman become one flesh and cannot be separated by human decree, nevertheless accepted a pastoral solution in the case of a marriage breakdown between an unbeliever and a believer. If the conversion of one of the partners had lead to disharmony and resulted in the pagan partner walking out of the marriage, the Christian should no longer be bound. It is not clear if this ruling was meant to give permission for re marriage, but it seems reasonable to conclude that it does, and tradition has lead to the Pauline Privilege being enshrined in Canon Law. The overriding consideration in such cases is that a state of wholeness ('peace') should prevail. The rules are complicated and the final decision rests with the Pope, enabling a dispensation to be granted in non-sacramental marriages. This is sometimes known as the Petrine Privilege.

The majority of petitions for annulments are made under new provisions in cases where there was 'a lack of due discretion', or 'incapacity to assume the obligation of marriage'. These extensions to Canon Law were made in the light of new knowledge of psychology. It had been asserted in the Vatican II Council that Church practice should be revised in the light of modern psychological research.

One person who has researched the situation of Catholics whose marriages have broken down or who are in second or invalid marriages, is Timothy Buckley, a Redemptorist priest, who sets out his findings in his book, *What Binds Marriage?* (published by Geoffrey Chapman, 1997). In his conclusions he says, "the anomalies, inconsistencies and injustices of the present pastoral situation have been highlighted repeatedly in this study" (page 165). Timothy Buckley goes on to say that the instincts of many Catholics, "tell them that the saving presence of Jesus must be able to reach into every situation, especially those that cry out to him because they are part of the very brokenness he came to redeem" (page 178). On this basis he believes that the instincts of the faithful are very close to the tradition of oikonomia in the Orthodox Church.

Oikonomia, the original meaning could be translated 'home economics', refers to the good ordering of a household. In the New Testament, oikonomia is usually translated as 'steward' or 'manager'. The well known parable of Jesus recorded in Luke 16 used to be known as the parable of the unjust steward, more recently described as the clever manager. In the parable, Jesus describes a manager who proved to be unsatisfactory and was given notice of dismissal. Realising he would soon lose his job, the man gave discounts on all outstanding bills, so people would remember he did them a good turn and might be helpful to him. Jesus commended the manager for his pragmatic approach.

As stewards of the household of faith, Orthodox bishops show a pragmatic approach in their pastoral care for people who have experienced marital breakdown. John Meyendorff, of Fordham University, in his book, *Byzantine Theology* (Mowbray's Edition, 1975), says that the Orthodox Church considers it inevitable that some marriages fail in the fallen world, "where man can accept grace and refuse it; where sin is inevitable, but repentance always accessible; where the Church's function is never to compromise the norms of the Gospel, but to show compassion and mercy to human weakness" (page 198). Timothy Ware asserts that when a marriage "has entirely ceased to be a reality, the Orthodox Church does not insist on the preservation of a legal fiction. Divorce is seen as an exceptional but necessary concession to human sin; it is an act of oikonomia ('economy' or dispensation) and of philanthropia (loving kindness), (page 302, *The Orthodox Church* by Timothy Ware, Pelican Books reprint 1981).

St Paul in his Epistle to the Ephesians describes God's management plan for the whole of creation: "a plan (oikonomia) for the fullness of time, to gather up all things in him (Christ), things in heaven and things on earth." This is the master plan: that everyone and everything shall be restored in Christ and brought to perfection. In accordance with this plan, the Orthodox Church sees its task as bringing sinners to repentance and restoration. Sacraments require human co-operation with the possibility of human failure, but repentance always allows a new beginning.

Although Orthodox Christians use the term divorce, they absolutely believe that marriage is indissoluble. The union having once been made remains for all time as part of eternal reality; but that union might in temporal time die, just as cells in the body die and are replaced. In the resurrection, everything which has made a person who she or he is, is raised, restored and glorified. We might say that in the Kingdom of God nothing is added, nothing taken away. Salvation is never quite completed this side of the grave; we are as yet 'a work in progress'.

Pastoral practice in the Orthodox Church for people seeking a second (even a third, but never a fourth) marriage begins with a process of compassion, repentance and forgiveness, after which an appropriate form of marriage service, with a declaration of penitence for past failure, is allowed.

In times past it was not clear if widows could marry again since sacraments have eternal reality. We recall the incident where the Sadducees asked Jesus about a woman whose husbands kept dying, and in accordance with religious law she married again after the death of each husband, seven times in all! "In the resurrection", the Sadducees asked, "whose wife will she be?" (Mark 12:23). In reply Jesus revealed that our mortal state is different from our eternal state, earthly processes are different from heavenly processes. When we affirm belief in the resurrection of the body, we do not mean that our mortal remains will be reassembled and preserved for ever in a heavenly museum, we mean that every feature of our life, from birth to death, will be transfigured in highest fidelity into a new and active life with God. Our mortal bodies are seen by the light of the sun; our immortal bodies will be suffused in the light of God. Jesus was wounded in his mortal body; his wounds are features of his eternal ministry.

All marriages are indissoluble.
Even irregular marriages are indissoluble.

Jesus was aware of the five marriages of the Samaritan woman he spoke to at the well (John 4: 1 to 26). He was aware of her present irregular relationship. Had she asked him, he would have given her life-giving water, the fountain of life springing up into eternal life. If Jesus was willing to meet the spiritual thirst of a woman with a history of irregular marriages, surely the Church should not withhold holy communion from those trying to begin again after a previous failed relationship.

11.

Gladly to Mass

We live in a water mill, a large rectangular stone building erected in 1851. We share the accommodation with our daughter, her husband and their two daughters. Like churches at the seaside, the place is packed in the holiday season with visitors: our eldest son, his wife, their two daughters; and our younger son, his wife and their two sons. Not to mention friends!

At 9.45 a.m. on Sundays we get into our car, my wife and me in the front, our grand daughters in the back, to go to Mass at Tenby. The journey in the car is the private space where we share our intimate conversation. It is soon apparent that children suffer a great many injustices. Parents are serious offenders, but teachers are even worse. Zola testifies, "On winter days, they force us out of our classrooms into the freezing playground, while they sit in their steamy classroom having cups of tea and chocolate biscuits." Yoko adds, "they repeatedly accuse us of having done things we haven't done. Punishments are given which are not deserved." Zola concludes, "there is nothing you can do about it. If you complain you are punished for being insolent."

The girls, young teenagers, explore politics with us. They appear to be left of their father who was a

Special Adviser to David Miliband. They are exasperated with their mother who says she quite likes David Cameron. Yoko thinks Cameron is bad for the country, but thinks Nick Clegg is worse because he promised students he would not charge tuition fees, but now he has put them up to £9,000! If she and Zola want to go to university (she is undecided, but Zola has fixed her sights on Cambridge) it is doubtful if their parents could afford to pay. Yoko calculates that if they can't afford to send her to university, perhaps her parents could afford to buy her a horse.

We often confess religious doubts. Zola says she believes in God for the time being because her parents believe, and she can make up her mind when she is older. Yoko has not shown her hand, but she is cross that she and Zola are not allowed to take Communion in the Catholic Church.

On the return journey, Mary and I are interested to hear what the girls think about the Mass. They say they like coming with us to Mass, assuring us that it is not because of lunch at the 'Blue Ball' afterwards, although that too is appreciated. Zola on the occasion when a visiting priest included talking to the children in his homily, said she thought the priest did not really understand children. On another occasion, when a priest claimed that over 80% of what you read in the newspaper is lies, Yoko queried his statistic. On a recent journey home, they said they preferred the Mass to the services we used to go to at our local URC chapel. They insisted that they liked the chapel and they liked the people who go to the chapel, but Zola said she prefers the Mass because there is more to see and do. Free Church services are sometimes boring, especially when the sermon goes on for more than twenty minutes. I was interested in Yoko's comment, "the Mass is well organised".

I have always avoided 'happy clappy' churches. There was nothing 'happy clappy' about the Mission Hall where I became a Christian. The whole service moved urgently towards the main event, the passionate sermon by Rev. William Barker which called for a decision: Sin and Damnation, or Christ and Salvation? Many Baptist churches now have 'praise bands', overhead projectors, 'power point' sermons, and all sorts of incongruous innovations. I deplore these developments. At the churches where I ministered, the services had a liturgical form, similar to that of the Mass. When I was no longer in pastoral charge, I found many Chapel services which included Holy Communion, left me disappointed because they were memorial ordinances, not the sacrament for which I yearned.

What is it like, going to Mass? It is different from going to any other church. Cradle Catholics are instantly at home. Even if they lapse for several years, they pick up the rituals without any hesitation. I am still like a raw recruit trying to keep in step. I enter the church at the same time as an Irish woman who genuflects deeply and crosses herself as she levels her gaze to the crucifix above the altar. I am still a learner, and too old to worship with my body without self consciousness. I hold on to the pew end, lower myself as best I can, while making the sign of the cross.

Evangelical Christians do not recognise the presence of God in buildings, art, or altar breads. God exists for them only in their hearts. I am glad that I can now acknowledge God in a church building full of signs of his presence. Catholics do not talk in the holy place, although it is usual to exchange an affectionate smile with a parishioner you know well, perhaps a kiss even. Preparing for worship, you kneel in your pew, cross yourself and start to pray.

Baptists, I am reminded, do not believe in sacred spaces; but Catholics do. God resides in churches where Jesus is present in the sacrament. If through sin, anxiety or grief, you lose the image of God: go into a Catholic church, in your need, look for the sanctuary light. God is there.

The Mass has a precise shape. The Liturgy of the Word begins with the invocation of the Holy Trinity, the Penitential Rite, and the Gloria. There follows a reading from the Old Testament, the Responsorial Psalm, the Epistle, the reading from the Gospel by the priest as the congregation stand. The homily and recitation of the Creed, is followed by bidding prayers.

The Liturgy of the Eucharist begins with the Offertory Procession. The Offertory Procession is a significant event in our local church, lead by two servers dressed in white, followed by children who have been in their Sunday School class. The Offertory Procession takes the bread and the wine up to the altar. The bread and wine, taken up by two people chosen at random, represent our everyday lives. The people chosen may be a nurse, a doctor, a policeman, a builder, or a public sector worker. They may be unemployed, retired, or working in the oil industry at Milford Haven. The significance is that our lives, with our various skills and weaknesses, our virtues and our sins, are being offered up to God. Whatever is well pleasing to God is a thank offering for all the blessings of this life, whatever is uninspiring in us and compromised by us, is to be 'lifted up' and transformed by the Word of God, the inspiration of the Holy Spirit, and the amazing grace of Jesus Christ.

The Offertory Procession was given a new impact for me in a Mass I attended at the Eglise Saint-Maurice at Lille, France. This church is a very long building, which has been ingeniously divided into two parts. The first half as you enter, has been constructed as an amphitheatre, rather like the Globe Theatre, in London, where Shakespeare's plays are performed. Sitting on the raised seats in an almost complete circle, you look towards the space just below, and just off centre. The cast of women and men standing in a circle (it is like a dramatic performance), include a leader, singers, two readers, two or three people who lead prayers and a priest. The first part of the Mass in this setting resembles a play reading. In many respects that is what the first part of the Mass is; it introduces the congregation to the themes of this week's worship, bringing together the Old Testament, Psalm, the Epistle and the Gospel. The priest gives a homily. This is a preparation for what will follow in the second part of the Mass, and 'lived out' in our daily lives at home, at work, and in our communities.

It was the Offertory Procession at Eglise Saint Maurice which was most dramatic. At the end of Part One of the Mass, two people came into the centre space, holding up a large, round loaf of bread and a flagon of wine. Several others followed with goblets (shaped like a chalice but with wide bowls). Gradually, the congregation, who had been sitting in the 'amphitheatre' seats, went down into the centre space and followed the 'cast' in a procession into the second half of the building. Here was the altar, and we all crowded round, we were practically ON the altar! This really brought home the concept of sacrifice. The priest saying the Eucharistic prayer, broke the bread into pieces, re-enacting the crucifixion of Jesus who was broken on the cross. The wine was poured from the flagon into the goblets, re-enacting the blood of Christ flowing freely to cleanse the souls of the worshippers. The bread and wine, now transformed at the hand and by the prayer of the priest, by the power of the Holy Spirit, became the body and blood of Christ, given to the faithful.

The Mass at our local church has not such a dramatic setting, but the congregation kneeling during the Eucharistic Prayer, is none the less devout, and the faithful going up in single file to the altar, similarly receive the body and blood of Christ. The once-for-all sacrifice of Christ on the cross at Calvary has, in the power of the Holy Spirit, been made contemporary with us, which is why we call this sacred mystery, the Sacrifice of the Mass.

There is a degree of difference between a Nonconformist minister and a Catholic priest. There is still some discussion of this matter. The Rev. Dr Arthur Deakin, who was Principal of the Bristol Baptist College when I was a student there, insisted that the difference between a Baptist minister and a lay person is simply functional, when a Baptist minister is no longer in pastoral charge, he/she is a lay person. Most Baptists, however, reject Deakin's view, and believe that ordination has a spiritual significance, imparting divine as well as denominational authority to the minister. The Catholic priest, by virtue of the sacrament of Holy Orders, acts in 'persona Christi Capitis', that is, Christ himself is present in the priest. This presence of Christ does not guarantee the character of the priest, although it does guarantee the power of the Holy Spirit in the sacramental actions of the priest.

What is it about the Mass which is so satisfying? In the first place, every word and action in the liturgy has been carefully researched to bring it into conformity with scripture, the Apostolic tradition, and the guidance of the Holy Spirit in the present. Secondly, there is satisfaction in following rituals common to Catholics throughout the world. Thirdly, the Mass draws back the curtain giving a glimpse of heaven, the saints and those who have gone before us in the faith. Finally, the service moves to the highest moment of all when the believer receives the body and blood of Christ, the food of eternal life.

After Sunday Mass, parishioners in many Catholic churches go to the Parish Hall where refreshments are served and there is the opportunity for socialising. What strikes me is that the parishioners are quite animated, rather like children being let out of school. That is, come to think of it, partly the explanation: there are two or three dozen children who have been to Mass and are now free to run and call out to each other. The adults, also strongly discouraged from talking in church, greet each other enthusiastically after Mass. I have a suspicion that Catholics are less inhibited than Baptists. It is obvious gambling is not frowned upon, as is evident by the raffle being conducted in support of church funds. There is a bookstall and various religious articles on sale, as well as refreshments being served. It is like a mini market, which might offend extreme Protestants who recall our Lord casting out traders in the Temple!

There is considerable diversity among the parishioners at St Teilo's in Tenby. Perhaps as many as a third are Irish, or of Irish descent. English out number the Welsh. Next in numerical strength are the Italians. There are a few Americans who work at the oil refinery at Milford Haven, and several Philippinos who work in the health and care systems. There are a few Indians, some Africans, and several people whose roots are in the Slavic nations (the proportion of Polish people is much higher in many Catholic churches). I guess that at St Teilo's in Tenby, there are not many rich people, but there are a few who are poor.

What are they like, these Catholics? Perhaps the fact that many have at some stage in life been strangers in Britain, means that the parishioners 'look out' for one another. Even in our short time in the parish, two families who were homeless, have been taken into people's homes for extended periods of time. When we were 'snowed in', people phoned to see how we were, and when Mary had a small operation, people were concerned and promised prayer. This is not unusual among friends, but we have found exceptional kindness.

I have found great blessing in the worship and fellowship of the Catholic Church, but there must be something more. Jesus said those who are truly happy, or blessed, are those whose greatest desire is to do what God requires. Does God require more than the salvation of my soul? What about working for justice and peace? What are the responsibilities for Christians towards civil society? The Gospel calls for more than worship at the altar, happy families, and kindness to neighbours.

12.

Evangelisation

When it became clear that no-one wanted to employ me as an octogenarian, and that Mary and I were going to have to live on a tight budget, we took forward a project begun in 1986 called 'Streetwise', providing drug education for professionals. We run these courses for people currently working with drug addicts, or preparing for this caring work among the most vilified members of society.

Otherwise, I am no longer in charge of anything. An agonising pain in my abdomen one night was a sharp reminder that none of us is ever, in reality, in control of our lives. I was admitted to hospital and underwent surgery for the removal of my gall bladder. Mary also has had to have surgery, and is waiting to see if she needs any further treatment. Mary's brother died recently, we spent the last night at his bedside while his life ebbed away. So we are aware of our mortality. Our life has narrowed considerably, and no longer being in charge of anything makes me like the great majority of people who are not managers, executives, or 'movers and shakers'. Now I can identify more fully with the diminution of life experienced by many people who are poor and whose circumstances are grim.

My circumstances in most respects are idyllic. I have chosen to live in Pembrokeshire, in an isolated spot, far from where the action is. Withdrawing from a hyper active ministry in a strategic centre of population in London, I have had the opportunity to look to my own spiritual needs. In London my priority was the work of the Kingdom of God. Now my priority is being incorporated into Christ and his Church. Perhaps that had always been my priority, but my busy life had hidden this from me. While I was in pastoral charge and involved in Kaleidoscope, it was unlikely that I would have thought of becoming a Catholic. Now I am retired, having already been in the habit of going to Mass and having a sacramental understanding of the Eucharist, it became likely that I would become a Catholic.

Having taken that step, I could easily become seduced by Catholic spirituality to spend the remainder of my life cultivating my soul. Mass at my local Church is a source of real comfort to me. The Holy Week services this year were very significant for me. Previously, various commitments and a bout of sickness had not allowed me to complete the whole series of devotions leading up to Easter; this year I was able to participate fully and with great benefit. The parish retreat on Caldey Island was also more meaningful to me this year, than the year before.

I miss the commitment to social justice which is a feature of the life of those Baptist churches in touch with their historic roots. The 'Nonconformist Conscience' still gives to many Baptists their 'moral compass'. Sr. Frances Makower in her book, *Faith or Folly* (DLT,

1989), describes her amazement when she studied the minutes of the John Bunyan Baptist Church monthly church meetings: "No question here of a division between spiritual and workaday life, or, more bluntly, between Christian commitment and social intervention. The minutes cover a wide range of topics, the methods of interrogation in Northern Ireland, immigration laws, capital punishment, the notion of a 'just war' (this in relation to the Falklands conflict), Sunday trading, etc. On the many occasions when the meeting reached consensus, decisions were made to write to the appropriate government ministers, the local MP, the local authorities – and the correspondence would be followed up. Thus, on more than one occasion, church members met the various authorities. It is heartening that this small group of seemingly ordinary people have so often felt compelled to voice the Christian position."

During my first parish retreat on Caldey Island when I had the opportunity to participate in the daily pattern of worship in the Cistercian monastery, there was a half hour when Michael Doyle, the Sacristan at St Teilo's Church, introduced the topic of Catholic Social Teaching. I think it fair to say, this topic did not fire the imagination of the group. More than a year later, I asked Michael if he had more information on this social teaching. I was delighted when after Mass the following Sunday, Michael gave me a carrier bag containing books and documents on Catholic Social Teaching. Moreover, the heavy underscoring of the text showed that Michael was fully informed and fully engaged with this aspect of Catholic faith. This teaching of the Church is to be found by anyone who is interested, but why is it not a prominent feature of parish life?

I asked Mary Cooper, a cradle Catholic and a GP, what she knew of Catholic Social Teaching. Mary explained that coming from a strong Catholic background in Ireland, she imbibed her Catholic faith as a child. She had a thorough grounding in Catholic teaching at her Primary School leading to First Communion. This teaching based on a concise version of the Catechism was learned by heart. She can recall the Bishop visiting her class and examining the children, asking each child a question from the Catechism and expecting the given answer. A section of Bible stories was taught, especially the Ten Commandments and the Gospels. Other teaching might be described as Church rules. She cannot recall being taught a formal body of social teaching called Catholic Social Teaching.

Peter Cooper, an artist and recent convert, expressed irritation with the Latin titles of the Pope's encyclicals. He felt disinclined to read documents using Latin phrases. He felt very strongly that this commitment to Latin was off putting. He thought the Catholic Church offered a way of looking at life which was an important corrective to much contemporary thinking. He would welcome more discussion of issues, rather than handed down, dogmatic teaching.

Part of the explanation for a lack of knowledge of Catholic Social Teaching is that this has been developed in recent times, before the older generation received their Catholic formation in childhood. It is unlikely that many Catholics would read *Gaudium et Spec*, a Latin document from the Vatican II Council which includes teaching about what it means to be human, about social justice, about the poor, and about peace. Previous Councils of the Church had been concerned with developing the Creed and other aspects of church life, but towards the end of Vatican II attention turned to the Church in the modern world. There is continuing debate among theologians as to what kind of constructive role the Church should play in political affairs, but at Vatican II the socio-economic order was put on the agenda. Perhaps parish priests, wishing to avoid controversy, do not like to comment on economic matters, but for those who have ears to hear, the prophetic voice of the Church is not silent.

If it is the case that many Catholics have not registered what recent popes have said about capitalism, Eric Hobsbawn certainly has! Hobsbawn, described by *The Spectator* as our greatest living historian, said of Pope John Paul II's criticism of untamed global markets: "the only person of global importance to condemn capitalism is the Pope."

Pope Benedict XVI in an encyclical has written: "If the market is governed solely by the principle of the equivalence in value of exchanged goods, it cannot produce the social cohesion that it requires in order to function well, without internal forms of solidarity and mutual trust, the market cannot completely fulfil its proper economic function. And today it is this trust which has ceased to exist, and the loss of trust is a grave loss." (*Caritas in Veritate* 35).

At a recent meeting of the Food and Agriculture Organisation of the United Nations, Pope Benedict denounced the way food is now being traded as a commodity: "How can we ignore the fact that food has become an object of speculation or is connected to movements in a financial market that, lacking in clear rules and moral principles, seems anchored on the sole objective of profit?" Food is sometimes hoarded to inflate the price, causing the poor to go hungry.

The bishops in England and Wales have indicated that they want to "deepen social engagement" by the Church. This can only be achieved if study and action groups dedicated to Catholic Social Teaching are to become a regular feature of parish life. The clergy are already overstretched by their duties at the altar and by pastoral work. This is a distinct work of the laity, which properly belongs to their Christian vocation. At a Mass to celebrate the closure of the Year of the Priest, in June 2010, Bishop Thomas Matthew of Menevia, referring to the duties of priests declared: "And to do all this, we cannot do it alone. There is another aspect of priesthood that complements the ordained priesthood. It is the priesthood of the laity. It is the priesthood conferred on all who are baptised."

The world has been shaken to its foundations by the collapse of financial institutions in the USA, Britain, Europe and most other countries. It is clear for all to see that this has happened not fortuitously, but because venerable financial institutions forgot honour, no longer traded honestly, but were motivated solely by greed. Bankers sold worthless stuff, in many cases selling stuff they did not own, intending to get

147

rid of it before it was time to pay! These are shameless merchants. Their immoral deeds cannot be described in temperate language: only biblical language is sufficient to pronounce judgement:

"Alas, alas, the great city,
  Babylon, the mighty city!
  For in one hour your judgement has come."

(Revelation, chapter 18).

Babylon in the book of Revelation refers to Rome. The event which triggered the vindictive outburst recorded in chapters 18 and 19 may have been the martyrdoms of St Peter and St Paul. The writer had been 'a partaker in the suffering' (Revelations 1:9), that is to say, the author had been in Rome in AD 69 when the city was sacked and burned. That is the probable historical background to Revelation. As it happened, Rome was spared for the time being from the judgement pronounced upon it. In AD 70 Jerusalem fell, and Rome became the new location for the leadership of the Church.

In such a way, it is to be hoped that the City of London, in the mercy of God, can be spared the judgment which might otherwise be pronounced. The scandalous wealth of the bankers and heads of multi national corporations who work in the city, and live in the most comfortable parts of London, are the focus of the anger many people feel at the austerity being forced upon them, and the injustice being suffered by the poor.

The Prime Minister has expressed his moral outrage at the actions of criminals in the four days of riots in London and other cities in the UK in August 2011; but everyone knows of the immoral and criminal behaviour of some MPs, bankers and hackers at News International. That News International had their man on their payroll in 10 Downing Street shows the dubiousness of operations at the heart of government.

The Coalition government has cut corporation tax, cut capital gains tax and greatly increased relief for business entrepreneurs. These huge tax breaks are morally justified if the government regulates the City, to ensure the money goes to create new jobs, and does not simply increase the incomes of top executives and investors at a time when many people are being forced to accept cuts in their take home pay of at least 10%. If it is found that unimaginable wealth continues to flow to the already rich, while the general public suffer cuts in wages and services, and the poor are left undefended, there will be justifiable anger, and the moral glue which ensures social cohesion will dissolve, and there will be profound public disillusionment.

The "decent hard working families", beloved of politicians at election times, should receive wages sufficient to provide a dignified standard of living, meeting not only their physical needs, but their social and cultural needs also. Academics, working independent of government, can calculate what is a proper Living Wage, or even a 'London Living Wage' (which might be equivalent to a Rural Living Wage if transport costs are taken into account). It is a matter of social justice that a proper living wage should be made the legal minimum.

Government action should be taken to stop the practice of non-executive directors sitting on each others' boards and voting each other increased salaries, regardless of the general state of public finances. Agreement between parties is not sufficient to justify morally the amount to be received as salary, or wages.

Under proposals of the Coalition government, many families on benefit will be priced out of social housing in better class areas of England. The new market-pegged social housing rents will be unaffordable for many families when the new cap on benefits comes into effect. Keith Exford, chief executive of Affinity Sutton, Britain's largest social housing provider, says, "Most people living in our accommodation in inner London are working, often in part-time or insecure jobs. They can't afford to commute to the jobs and public transport is not available at 4 a.m. in the morning when they are coming in to clean offices. Do we want whole sections of our cities to be like Paris, only for the rich?"

I see a fissure opening up in our society. The middle class will make strenuous efforts to get on the rich side; doing everything possible to give their children a good education, to go to a good university, in order to gain entrance to a profession, providing sufficient income for a mortgage to buy a house, to enable them to marry a suitable partner! Those of the middle class who don't make it, face the prospect of their children, burdened with debts, having a lower standard of living than their parents. With so much being transferred to those who can afford to pay, fewer people will be able to enjoy a good life.

My concern about a fissure in British society, could develop into a fear of a chasm opening up, if radical proposals of the Coalition government to change social housing into temporary accommodation are taken forward. The pleasant Local Authority estate in Southend-on-Sea, where I served in my first pastorate, consisted of spacious semi detached houses with front and back gardens. People had a sense of pride in the estate, and certainly no stigma was attached to living there. There was a small criminal element, as there is in any class of society, but there was no threat from anti-social behaviour. Under the Thatcher government, these desirable residencies were sold off to owner occupiers, with the Local Authority being left with only poor stock. Some Local Authority housing estates became notorious, and Rachmanism flourished at the lower end of the 'housing market'. If the poor are now to be housed in temporary accommodation, children will be brought up with no sense of place of birth and belonging to a community. They will indeed be 'feral', having no real homes.

I can remember my parents' shock when at the end of the war, Winston Churchill was rejected at the general election. It soon became apparent who had done this. Men and women returning from the services were determined not to come home to the former class ridden society, with the rich and privileged being firmly in charge. They remembered what Churchill had done to the miners in South Wales. There had been a unity of purpose in the war, and people had come together to fight for freedom. (You might call this 'solidarity', or to give it another name in Catholic

Social Teaching, 'the common good'.) Although the finances of the nation were in a perilous state at the time, there was a sense of 'victory' in the air. This optimism gave birth to the Welfare State which benefited the general public greatly. The estate I described in Southend-on-Sea was a product of that era.

The reforms to the Welfare State being proposed by the Coalition government to deal with the immoral situation of people being made dependent upon social benefits, are long overdue. It is a duty of government to help the unemployed to find work and employment. The idea that work should always pay is a good one, as long as the minimum wage is a proper living wage, and that there is not a hidden purpose simply to reduce the already critically low level of benefits.

The key concept in Catholic Social Teaching is solidarity. "Solidarity is manifested in the first place by the distribution of goods and the remuneration for work. It also presupposes the effort for a more just social order." (*Catechism of the Catholic Church*). Without doubt, this teaching is needed in our times. Human solidarity, I suspect, is at the heart of all true religions, Christian and non-Christian alike. For Christians, our Lord Jesus Christ supremely exemplifies solidarity by becoming flesh, by becoming truly human as we should be, and reconciling us to God by his atoning death and glorious resurrection.

Jesus calls his disciples to interpret the signs of the times, to be busy doing the work of the Kingdom of God, to be mindful of his return in glory, when God will separate the evil from the good and judge the living and the dead. This is the vision of the Kingdom of God. The Church is the agent of the Kingdom. The Church is a means to that End. The End is the redemption of the world, when the kingdoms of this world are to become the kingdoms of our God, and of his Christ; and he shall reign for ever and ever.

Eschatological passages contained in both the Old and New Testaments, concerning death, judgement, heaven and hell, were used sometimes in the past to frighten people into religious practice, but the real purpose of prophecy is to give a perspective on life which is inspired by belief in God. Serious journalists attempt to provide analysis and comment upon contemporary events, but the biblical prophets were more radical in that they made no attempt to accommodate their understanding of events to what might be regarded as 'realistic', 'achievable', or 'politically practical'. More like artists and musicians, prophets were called to show things in the searching light of God's truth, and leave the practical outworking of that vision to those in authority. Elijah, Amos, Micah, Haggai and Joel, and many others, were a radical wing independent of the establishment, who spoke the Word of God and shone a powerful light upon their society: showing the moral features in black and white.

The prophet Joel spoke of sons and daughters fulfilling this divine vocation, old ones dreaming dreams and young ones seeing visions, even slaves, the humblest of the humble, being able to see right from wrong. (Joel 2:28).

The Elder John, on the Isle of Patmos (Revelation 1:9) saw with vivid clarity the events unfolding in his day in the light of eternity. The gift of the Holy Spirit on the day of Pentecost enabled the Apostles and the faithful to speak the Word of God. This is still an important part of the ministry of the Church today: to show what is really happening, without any pretence of understanding the situation in all its complexity, nevertheless proclaiming the moral truth about contemporary society.

This is a KAIROS (the biblical Greek word for a time of critical importance), a moment of truth in human affairs. The Middle East is in a state of violent revolution, whole populations no longer willing to submit to the injustice of oppression they have suffered for a long time. The European Union is in turmoil: Germany doing her best to bring about order and stability, but in danger of being seen as imposing debilitating conditions of austerity upon the populations of Greece, Italy and Spain. France has been allied to Germany in the attempt to create a greater European Union, but in choosing an economy based on agriculture, and allowing Germany to choose manufacturing, there is a danger of economic rivalry between France and Germany. The United Kingdom has an increasing population of unemployed young people who are showing a growing sense of exclusion which is of concern. Teachers, nurses, public service workers, transport workers, large sections of the workforce, are all rejecting the political settlement which allows top executives to increase their pay by 49% at the same time when most people are facing hardship, and the poor are fearful of having barely enough to live on.

The Archbishop of Canterbury and the Bishop of London have identified themselves alongside the anti-capitalist protestors outside St Paul's Cathedral. It is unclear what Archbishop Vincent Nichols would do if the protestors camped on the piazza in front of Westminster Cathedral, but Catholic Social Teaching calls for solidarity with the poor and this suggests Catholics might need to decide where they stand.

When at the end of the 1960's the Baptist Church I pastored in Kingston-upon-Thames opened its doors to members of the youth movement who were at that time rebelling against consumerism and globalisation, there was considerable disquiet felt by some traditionalists in our own congregation, and even more so amongst neighbouring Baptist congregations. The fear was that we were about to compromise their understanding of the Gospel, and they imagined there would follow a degeneration in our worship and spiritual life. They were wrong. The 150 or so, swelling to 350 at one time, coming to our Kaleidoscope Project daily, did not trample upon our sacred scriptures nor desecrate our holy place. On the contrary, the encounter with these radical young people demanded our closer attention to the Gospel, and the inadequacy of our human resources increased our dependence on Christ in the Eucharist. As a result, we experienced a renewal in our worship and a strengthening of our congregation.

The challenge facing the small Baptist congregation in Kingston provides a demonstration of the KAIROS which occurred in the first decades of the early church, particularly involving James, Peter and Paul together with their co-workers. When Paul opened the doors of the Church to the Gentiles, there was a theological and pastoral crisis. Who is, and who is not, acceptable to God? Paul was seriously engaged in the theological task of formulating a catechism of the Church: his epistles (encyclicals if you like) to the Romans and to the Galatians especially, were intended to guard the tradition of faith which he had received from the Lord Jesus Christ, and which should stand for every age. What then of those Jewish religious and cultural traditions, such as circumcision, dietary regulations and a multiplicity of other rules which the first Christians still observed but which were no longer appropriate for those coming into the church as a result of Paul's evangelising missions? Thank God, the apostles meeting together in the Council of Jerusalem, were able to separate out what was eternally valid, and what applied to a former dispensation.

To me it seems inevitable that if the Catholic Church seriously engages in a mission of evangelisation, and seriously intends to engage with others in the development of economic and social policies for the common good, there will come a KAIROS, a critical moment, when the Church will need urgently to decide between what is ordered by God for all ages, and what is ecclesiological, that is to say a feature of church life which might need to be reformed. If a large number of lapsed Catholics are to return to the Church, they would include many divorced and re-married people, homosexuals, and women questioning whether a male only priesthood has more to do with the roles for women in former times, than with the teaching of

Jesus. A younger generation of Catholics would expect more active participation in the life of the Church, otherwise they will seek fulfilment elsewhere. Such challenges to the settled state of Church life should not be anticipated with alarm. Sister Frances Makower in the concluding part of her book, *Faith or Folly?* (DLT 1989) describes her experience of close encounter with unchurched young people: "Thus I arrived at Kaleidoscope with some strange ideas about Gospel values which had more to do with middle-class behaviour than with the teaching of Jesus. Those ideas were immediately challenged, because Kaleidoscope is a place of such integrity that it acts as a mirror in which motives, gut reactions and feelings are reflected with uncomfortable clarity." Uncomfortable certainly, but also transforming.

Many churches in all denominations experience an ebbing away of vitality. Opening the doors to new-comers means more than simply offering a welcome. Churches need to offer unconditional hospitality. There needs to be a joyful anticipation of surprises and a delight in new companionships.

The members of the first English Baptist Church covenanted together "to walk in all His ways, made known or to be made known, whatsoever it might cost, the Lord assisting." They did not think they had reached finality, but they were ready to embrace what-ever might yet be revealed. Some truths are handed down to us from the past, other truths must be dis-covered. St Matthew (13:52) records the saying of Jesus: "Therefore, every scribe who has been trained for the kingdom of heaven is like the master of a household who brings out of his treasure what is new and what is old."

Transformation occurs when there is a fusion of the past and the future. Unless such fusion takes place, the species dies out. May Christ, according to his promise, continue to guard and guide his Church in these critical times.